QUINOA
THE Supergrain

"It shimmers like white caviar." Mary Estella, professional chef and author, New York, New York

"Quinoa (*keen' wa*). Keen what?" Jeffrey Markel, retired importer, Motueka, New Zealand

"A *real* mouthful." Charlie Papazian, brewmaster and publisher, Lafayette, Colorado

"It's very nourishing." Michio Kushi, macrobiotic diet teacher and author, Brookline, Massachusetts

"It becomes addictive." Orlando P. Lloyd, Gestalt therapist, Arlington, Virginia

"I like to take it backpacking because it's quick cooking." Rita Thangaras, physical therapist, Big Sur, California

"It gives me lots of energy." Jane Quincannon, fashion model, Miami Beach, Florida

"Of all my (non-allergen) foods, this is the only one my husband likes." Nickie Dumke, mother and homemaker, Louisville, Colorado

"Following my colostomy it was the easiest grain to digest." Stuart Mace, farmer and teacher, Aspen, Colorado

"It's got little halos." Monique Risi, age 6, Lima, Peru

QUINOA THE Supergrain

ANCIENT FOOD FOR TODAY

Rebecca Wood
Author of *The Whole Foods Encyclopedia*
Foreword by Nikki and David Goldbeck

Japan Publications, Inc.

Photo credits:

Andre Ulrich, Barbara Svenning, Gabriel Howearth and Hugh D. Wilson

Distributors:
UNITED STATES: *Kodansha International/USA, Ltd., through Harper & Row, Publishers, Inc., 10 East 53rd Street, New York, N. Y. 10022.* SOUTH AMERICA: *Harper & Row, Publishers, Inc., International Department.* CANADA: *Fitzhenry & Whiteside Ltd., 195 Allstate Parkway, Markham, Ontario, L3R 4T8.* MEXICO AND CENTRAL AMERICA: *HARLA S. A. de C. V., Apartado 30-546, Mexico 4, D. F.* BRITISH ISLES: *Premier Book Marketing Ltd., 1 Gower Street, London WCIE 6HA.* EUROPEAN CONTINENT: *European Book Service PBD, Strijkviertel 63, 3454 PK De Meern, The Netherlands.* AUSTRALIA AND NEW ZEALAND: *Bookwise International, 1 Jeans Street, Beverley, South Australia 5007.* THE FAR EAST AND JAPAN: *Japan Publications Trading Co., Ltd., 1–2–1, Sarugaku-cho, Chiyoda-ku, Tokyo 101.*

First edition: April 1989

LCCC 87–82908
ISBN 0–87040–780–5

Printed in U.S.A.

This book is dedicated to the Aymara and Quechua of the South American altiplano. Five thousand years ago their ancestors domesticated and glorified a plant called quinoa (keen′ wa).

We cannot live harmlessly. To live we must daily break the body and shed the blood of Creation. When we do this knowingly, skillfully, reverently, it is a sacrament. When we do it ignorantly, greedily, clumsily, destructively, it is a desecration. In such a desecration we condemn ourselves to spiritual and moral loneliness, and others to want.

WENDELL BERRY
from *The Gift of the Good Land*

Contents

Foreword

You are about to begin a lesson on food in history, a travelogue, a culinary adventure, and one woman's personal saga. All of this will be accomplished in company with one of the world's ancient foodstuffs, the grain quinoa.

Rebecca Wood recognizes the cultural rôle food plays, and this makes QUINOA THE SUPERGRAIN richer and more essential than most cookbooks. Before you even begin to cook, you feel a relationship developing between yourself, Rebecca, the ancient Incas, and the modern-day Indians of Bolivia and Peru, as well as the contemporary "quinoa pioneers" in the Rocky Mountains. You will find yourself in the high Andes, and then suddenly back again with Rebecca in the kitchen.

However, romanticism does not get in the way of practicality in these pages. The nutritional aspects of quinoa, as presented here are most inspiring. Regarding optimum food and nutrition, we subscribe to four simple tenets:

- Rely on historically selected foods, i.e. those foods our ancestors ate, eaten in similar proportions.
- Reduce intake of food components which do not exist in nature and to which our bodies are unaccustomed.
- Vary food selection to maximize the chance of receiving unknown, as well as known nutrients.
- Eat foods as close to their natural form as possible.

In addition to its specific nutrient profile, quinoa fits all four of these criteria. In a wheat-centered culture like ours, quinoa adds to the list of grain foods that can fulfill the essential need for variety. Moreover, quinoa accomplishes this in a most pleasurable way.

When it comes to rating foods, most people judge first by taste. In our North American markets, where access to different foods is almost limitless, there is little reason to eat foods that do not offer some degree of pleasure. Thus no food, no matter how virtuous, can thrive here without the benefit of proper presentation.

Often we find that cookbooks designed around a specific food are no more than a collection of familiar recipes with the featured item "inserted" into the formula. In contrast, Rebecca Wood has created innovative recipes that capitalize on quinoa. Covering every meal, and every course, the recipes are imaginative and capture the unique qualities of the grain. As an additional incentive to cooks in today's busy households, preparation is uncomplicated; directions clear and concise. The numerous variations enable us each to adapt the dishes to our individual eating styles and add a personal touch.

With quinoa and Rebecca Wood's guidance in this comprehensive volume, you can "travel" (even if you never leave your own table) throughout the intriguing Andean altiplano.

NIKKI and DAVID GOLDBECK
Authors of *American Wholefoods Cuisine* and *The Goldbeck's Guide to Good Food*

Preface

Last October at New York's JFK airport the cold rain did not dampen my spirits. I was on my way south of the equator, to where the sun had gone for the winter. Peru and Bolivia beckoned me. Here was the cradle of quinoa (keen′ wa) cultivation. For thousands of years prior to the conquistadores, the Indians of the *altiplano* (high plains of the Andes mountains) revered their main staple, quinoa. Among other things, I hoped that this trip would help me understand how quinoa contributed to the amazing physical endurance, refined sense of beauty, and highly developed Andean civilizations.

Some people advised me not to travel alone in Peru, but I had brushed up on my Spanish, had filled my backpack pouches with little gifts of flashlights (most Indians are without electricity) and balloons, and I was ready to go. Whatever lay in store held the promise of high adventure.

I recalled the first time I had tasted quinoa. Little did I know then where it would lead me. In 1983 in Boulder, Colorado, I heard rumors about the availability of a new grain. It had the improbable name of quinoa. As a food consultant, writer, and culinary instructor, I was curious—but skeptical about it. The stories of quinoa's unique flavor and seemingly magical properties increased. I tracked down a phone number for this mystery food. The friendly voice of Stephen Gorad invited me to visit the Quinoa Corporation offices and see for myself.

The next day I was on a quiet street knocking on the door of a modest Boulder office with a side-yard entrance. The front rooms housed the graphics business of Gorad's partner, Don McKinley. In a windowless back room I encountered quinoa. It was obvious which business paid the rent. This reality did not subdue Gorad's, McKinley's, and David Cusack's dream of introducing this ancient grain to North America.

In a small pot on his office hot plate Gorad brought water to a boil. He added a pinch of salt and some of this new foodstuff. While it simmered, he quietly talked about the politics, history, magic, and mystery of quinoa. By the time it was cooked, my doubts had dissipated. With my first taste, I was hooked. Within two years, their modest enterprise would move uptown. Several other national companies would market quinoa and numerous quinoa products—and this would be just the beginning.

I returned from South America five months ago. While there I savored quinoa *humintas* (tamales) wrapped in corn husks which I purchased for a pittance from a shy Indian child. I marveled at snow-capped, 21,500-foot Mt. Illampu. My breath was taken by its reflection in the waters of the world's bluest and highest navigable lake, Titicaca. In the thin altiplano air I dreamed timeless dreams. At the miraculous Incan temple, Machu Picchu, I reflected on the potent sustaining force quinoa provided for its builders, priestesses, and god-king. And I fell in love with the gentle Indians.

One vivid recollection of my altiplano sojourn is of sound. I can almost hear the joyous lilting folk music and the immense, silent village plazas and countryside. It is a restful quiet, a quiet randomly punctuated by the people's sweet laughter.

In appreciation for their gift of quinoa, for their beauty, and for their need, 50 percent of my profits from this book are pledged to organizations working with and for the altiplano Indians. These organizations include: Freedom from Hunger Foundation, Habitat for Humanity, Institute for Food and Development Policy, and Mother Teresa's Sisters of Charity. Since the use of minor food crops—such as quinoa—improves global economy and health, it is a pleasure to offer this book. May it serve Americans in both the northern and the southern hemispheres.

REBECCA WOOD
Crestone, Colorado
March, 1988

Acknowledgments

Since 1983 I have enjoyed preparing quinoa for my family because it is delicious, it is also strengthening and versatile. The opportunity to create the first book about quinoa is a gift and a responsibility. I wish to serve the topic well and hope to serve you, my reader. I am hopeful that our interest in quinoa will empower South American Andean Indians and elevate quinoa's status.

One problem with presenting a book on quinoa is that little is known or written about it. Some of the available information is contradictory. A similar problem presents itself with recounting the story of the quinoa-eating peoples. Relative to the rest of the world, rural South American history is obscure. Herein, I present the most current information available; and I claim full responsibility for any errors.

I enjoy carving out a block of time and diving into an all-consuming project—like writing this book. The ability for me to "produce" a book, however, is totally dependent upon the efforts of many. For the numerous friends, neighbors, family, scientists and food professionals who have assisted me, with both desk and kitchen research, I am indeed grateful.

Special thanks to Stephen Gorad, founder of the Quinoa Corporation, Boulder, Colorado, who introduced me to quinoa and who has generously given his time, data, resources and friendship. Thanks also to the people involved in cultivating and introducing quinoa to the United States who have inspired me—David Cusack (deceased), Stuart Mace, Hanne Strong, John McCamant, Gabriel Howearth, Tom and Lillian McCracken, Ernie New, Duane Johnson, and Emigdio Ballon.

Thank you for sharing your research: David L. Browman, Johan Krug, Bruce D. Smith, Juan Risi, Noel D. Vietmeyer, and Hugh D. Wilson.

A special thanks to Barbara Svenning, my cooking confidante of twenty years. Her light, sensitive culinary touch enhances many of these recipes. Thanks to all those who have suggested recipes and/or helped test them: Johnna Albi, Felipe Rojas-Lombardi, Sally Kane, Pamela Bertin, Megan Jarvis, Anne Silver Philleo, Suzanne Foote, Helen Sandler, Susan Carskadon, Kim Moore, Andrea Aronson, Thea Tenenbaum, and Isabel Mace.

Thanks to my first-class editing and publishing team: Meg Seaker, Margot Williams, Yoshiro Fujiwara and Japan Publications.

For those who sampled upwards of five quinoa dishes a day: Lloyd Alexander, Mir and Ryan Garvy, and my children, Roanna, Asa and Elizabeth Greenwood, thank you.

PART I

The STORY of QUINOA

1. From My Kitchen Window

From my kitchen window I look out onto the high mountain desert. My home, nestled amidst juniper and piñon, abuts the dramatic Sangre de Cristo mountains. This range, the most vertical in the United States, has rugged peaks jutting over 6,500 feet from the 7,500-foot valley floor. Fifty miles west, across the arid San Luis Valley, lie the La Garita Mountains. Between these two mountain ranges the predominant vegetation is yucca, saltbush and cactus. The most prevalent evening sound is the yapping of coyotes. There is cattle ranching nearby, potato farming and buffalo ranching farther south. The land that stretches before me is relatively intact, uncultivated and seemingly inhospitable. In this expanse, my eye is continually drawn to one spot a few miles west.

Last spring I watched winds blowing dust as a tractor plowed a 30-acre plot. The exposed dark earth contrasted boldly with the muted desert tones. Within weeks the soil was touched with pubescent green glimmers. Daily it became more intense, more gold in color and depth. By July it was brashly green. Now, as harvest nears, the field, viewed from my window, glimmers and shimmers gold—a robust, lusty gold.

The crop is the grain quinoa (keen'wa). This modest field bears one of the first commercial quinoa crops grown in the United States. When green, the plant looks like a cross between spinach and sorghum. In the field of mature quinoa, I walk up the rows and am astounded by the colors. The five-foot stalks are a flamboyant fuschia. The heavily laden seed heads are a boggling color display—blood-orange red, creamy ivory, brash purple, bee-pollen yellow, jade green, earthy ocher, ruby rose, ethereal lavender, pumpkin orange, raspberry red, and ebony black. These brazen colors have the rich luster of pure earth tones; otherwise they would be reduced to garish psychedelic hues. To my eyes, quinoa is the most comely crop ever seen in a field.

Quinoa thrives in drought conditions at elevations of 10,000 feet and higher. This chenopod and its near-relative, cañihua, are adapted to thin air, high radiation levels, hot sun, subfreezing temperatures and poor, sandy, alkaline soil. Few other food crops could survive such adversity.

Each quinoa seed head has an abundance of seed, enough to plant one-fourth of an acre. (The seed from one wheat head will plant a 30-foot row.) Take a few seeds and rub, or wash off, their bitter, inedible saponin. This eliminates their glorious color, but leaves kernels the size and color of sesame seeds with lentil-like shapes.

The periphery of each disk-shaped grain is bound with a narrow germ or embryo. When cooked, the white, wispy, crescent embryo separates from the seed and offers the teeth a delicate crunch. The translucent grain melts in your mouth. This texture contrast is delightful. Quinoa's flavor (after the bitter saponin is removed) is slightly grain-sweet with a tangy-toned aftertaste. It is not heavy and sticky like other grains. It invites seasonings which can run the gamut from mild to wild. In the bowl, quinoa glistens like tiny jewels.

Quinoa (*Chenopodium quinoa* Willd.) is found in the *Chenopodiaceae*, or Goosefoot Family, which is so-named because their tri-lobed leaves look like a goose's foot. This category includes beets, chard, and the various spinach varieties.

The genus *Chenopodium* contains about 250 species, mostly weedy herbs found throughout the world. In the United States we call several species lamb's quarters or pigweed. In Great Britain we find another wild green named Good King Henry. Although this book deals with quinoa, it touches upon some close relatives.

Quinoa is not a new-fangled, low-cal food synthesized from wood chips. It is not a cure-all health-food supplement. Quinoa is more than a *nouvelle cuisine* experience to titillate jaded palates. Quinoa is a food staple. For centuries quinoa has been the "daily bread" for whole cultures in the Western Hemisphere. A chenopod near-relative was the pre-maize staple for some North American peoples. Today's "introduction" of quinoa to the United States is almost a reintroduction, a spiraling back.

In addition to including recipes for its use, this book examines the mystique, history, and use of quinoa and some of its unique characteristics:

- Quinoa has an amazing nutritional profile. and is therefore called a "supergrain."
- Quinoa is a high-endurance, aerobic efficiency food.
- People with cereal grain allergies can base their diets on quinoa.
- Quinoa has great potential as a food crop for arid Third World countries.
- It was revered as the sacred mother grain by the Incas.
- Some report that quinoa consumption enhances their psychic abilities and spirituality.

In order to examine these claims for quinoa, we must first look at the role of grains in human history.

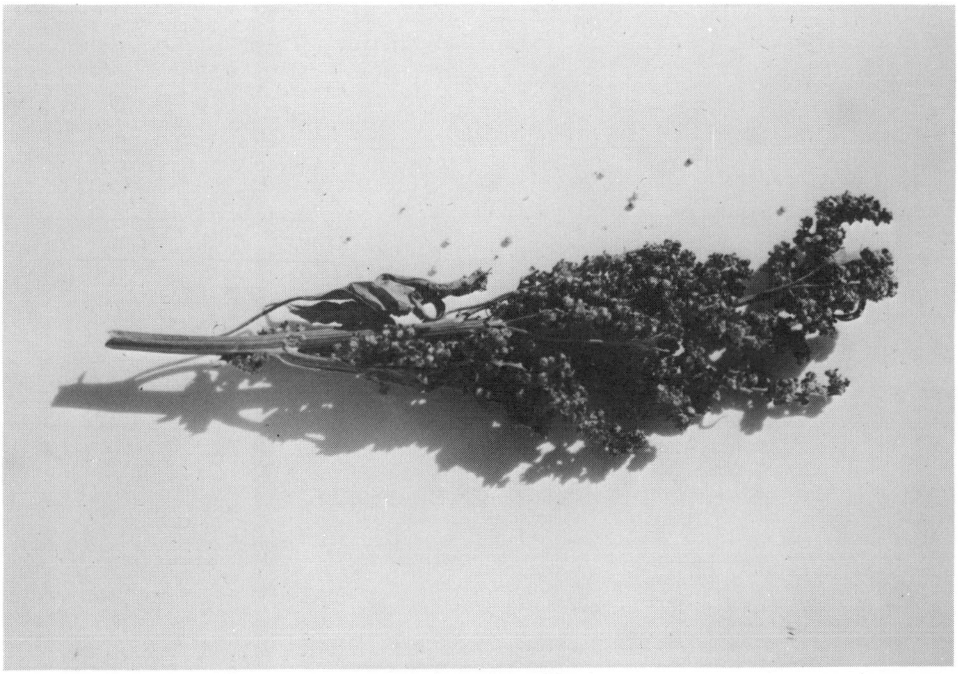

Stalk of dried quinoa

2. Grains and Civilization

The visual aid called for here is a handful of quinoa. If you do not have quinoa, use another whole grain such as wheat, brown rice, millet, or buckwheat. Oatmeal or corn grits will not work because they are broken; neither will white rice because it is refined.

Pour the quinoa (or other grain) into a shallow bowl. Now, have a long and close look at all those little seeds. What you are looking at is potentially hundreds of distinct plants. Each tiny unit miraculously contains both the fruit and seed. Each grain's DNA is encoded with the survival experience of millenia. Plant quinoa seed, and it can grow into a five-foot-high plant with over 100,000 new kernels. One pound of this seed—a mere four cups—will sow an acre. One acre can yield up to 2,000 pounds or more. For a traditional Andean altiplano family of ten, this much quinoa would easily provide a year's staple nourishment. All from a single handful of grain.

Whole grains, like quinoa, are indeed a gift. The grains which belong to the grass family include: barley, corn, Job's tears, millet, oats, rice, rye, sorghum, teff, and wheat. The leafy grains (those which are not grass family members) include: amaranth, buckwheat, and quinoa.

Early people were hunters and foragers. Their life expectancy seldom reached into their forties. Cultivating crops gave them a reliable food supply and thus a longer life.[1] Production of home-grown grains necessitated greater social organization. The staff of life for each of the so-called "high" civilizations invariably was a grain.*

It has been observed that breakfast during the golden age of Greece was a kind of barley gruel. Lunch was a barley dish, and supper consisted also of barley.

The Beginning of Culture: The principal crops of the cultivating people were the grains. They were their primary dietary staples and underpinned their social, economic, and religious systems. Grain foods were universally revered as essential to life. In addition to human sustenance, the grain plants were used as building materials, animal fodder, for clothing and fuel. The grains have made the cultural evolution of mankind possible.

Each civilization has considered its specific regional grain to be its staff of life. The Greek goddess Demeter was responsible for grain and agriculture. The Romans called her Ceres, from which comes our word cereal. The Roman gladiators called themselves *hordearii*, or "barley men," because they believed that barley gave them strength.

The Lord's Prayer begins its supplications with "Give us this day our daily bread."

---

* The relatively infrequent historical examples of non-grain eating peoples include: Australian aborigines who had no agriculture; peoples in the sub-arctic where grains do not grow; some North American plains Indians with societal prohibitions against planting; and some peoples in tropical areas where root or tuber crops were the primary staples.

In Jewish law the consumption of grain is equated with a meal and requires appropriate prayers. The Japanese Emperor annually makes a ritual planting of rice on the Imperial grounds. The Inca Emperors planted the first quinoa with a golden spade. According to Charles B. Heiser, in the book, *Of Plants and People:*

> Myths accounting for the origins of food plants (and the people themselves) are widespread among archaic people . . . and in many such myths the people themselves come from plants.[2]

The early religions of people the world over are indeed inextricably intertwined with agriculture. As grains have been our primary staple, they are among the most revered of foods. This is not to say that flesh foods were not valued. However, in most cultures meat, poultry, fish, and dairy products were secondary foods to grains. In many instances, meat was reserved for the nobility, the empowered classes, and for special feast days.

Grains Provide Superior Nutrition: It is most fortunate that grains are humanity's staple. They come closer than any other vegetable crop to providing an adequate diet. Grains contain all the major nutrient groups needed by the body—carbohydrates, protein, fats, vitamins and minerals. Historically, grains have sustained humanity; today they continue to do so for most of the world's populations. In parts of China, for example, rice makes up 70 percent of the average person's daily diet.

Most grains are deficient in the amino acid lysine which means that their protein profile is incomplete. Beans and other legumes are high in lysine and, therefore, provide an ideal grain complement for together they provide whole usable protein. (Conversely, grains are high in the essentials methionine and cystine in which beans are deficient.)

The tried-and-true practices of ethnic cuisines demonstrate the innate compatibility of grains and beans. Without knowing about amino acids and protein balance, intuitive cultures have "known" to combine beans and grains in endless variations. In the south, various beans are refried to go with tortillas, in the Far East rice is traditionally served with tofu (or tempeh or dahl), in the Middle East pita bread is filled with hummus (a chickpea and sesame blend), in Middle Europe rye bread and fava beans are a pair, in the Mediterranean, *fagoli* (beans) and pasta are a must for a minestrone soup, and so the list continues. Each ethnic cuisine is rich in examples of grains combined with beans to form a complete protein complement.

Wheat was not always the principal European grain. Rye thrives in cold climates and is still prominent in Scandinavian and Russian ethnic cuisines. Oats prefer the cold and damp and so are the "national grain" of Scotland. Buckwheat and barley are likewise each suited to specific ecological niches, so they also have regional popularity.

The grains of non-European cultures are prominent in their local social and religious life. African peoples enjoyed wheat, sorghum, numerous varieties of millet, and other grains which are barely known today. One such is Teff. Eastern civilizations ate rice, millet, barley, buckwheat, wheat, and lesser-known cereals such as Job's tears, branyard millet and *hie.*

With such a wealth of grains elsewhere in the world, it is curious that corn, as is popularly believed, is the "only" recognized traditional grain of the Western hemisphere. Histories occasionally mention other idigenous American grains—wild rice, amaranth and "wild seeds." Most people have yet to hear of quinoa, the best kept agricultural secret in 400 years.

The Health Effects of Declining Grain Consumption: Within the last several generations the principal food of affluent peoples has changed from cereal grains to animal foods. In a few short decades, we have made a radical dietary shift. The decrease in grain consumption directly correlates to affluence. "A national survey showed that for every 10-percent rise in household income, there was a corresponding 5-percent decline in the purchase of rice, pasta, and corn meal . . ."[3] presumably because ordinary food is considered food for the poor.

Many authorities correlate the modern American diet with the increase in degenerative disease. These early voices, including C. W. Post, John Harvey Kellogg, Gaylord Hauser, Robert Rodale, Sr., and Adelle Davis, were relegated to the realm of food faddism and even quackery. Until, that is, a landmark study in 1977 which irrefutably connected dietary practices with health. *Dietary Goals for the United States* was prepared by the U.S. Senate Select Committee on Nutrition and Human Needs. It encouraged increased whole grain consumption and decreased consumption of animal proteins, salt, fats and highly refined carbohydrates. To the mainstream medical and scientific communities, these recommendations appeared to be visionary. Today they are commonplace.

Five years later, the National Academy of Sciences' 1982 report *Diet, Nutrition and Cancer* presented a survey of the scientific data correlating cancer and diet. Since then the American Cancer Society and the National Cancer Institute have recommended a whole-grain and vegetable-based diet. The American Heart Association (which now serves brown rice at its annual banquet) has followed suit as have various other national and state health agencies.

Today the often heard expression, "you are what you eat," is an accepted truism. As a nation, it is apparent that we are not thriving on our highly refined convenience food and rich gourmet foods. People are becoming aware that eating a healthful diet may help prevent degenerative diseases and even ammeliorate them. It is common knowledge today that diet plays a significant role in maintaining health and preventing disease, whether it is acne, diabetes, or AIDS.

In addition to their preventive properties, grain-based diets may have curative or regenerative effects. Nathan Pritikin, who revolutionized our understanding of heart disease, recommended a predominantly grain diet. Anthony Sattilaro, M.D., in his book, *Recalled by Life*, details how a grain-based diet was key in curing his terminal prostate cancer. Michio Kushi and Martha C. Cottrell, M.D., document how a grain-based diet stabilizes AIDS victims in *AIDS: Macrobiotics and Natural Immunity* (Japan Publications, 1989).

Additional proponents of increased grain consumption include: John A. McDougall, M.D. and Mary A. McDougall (*The McDougall Plan*), Nathan Pritikin (*Pritikin Program*), Jane Brody (*Good Food Book*), Robert Haas (*Eat to Win*), Annemarie Colbin (*Food and Healing*), Gary Null (*The Egg Project*), and Laurel Robertson, *et al.* (*Laurel's Kitchen*). There is a growing list of medical doctors, holistic health-care practitioners, nutritionists, food writers, and sports nutritionists who encourage whole grain consumption for health.

Grains and Radiation: New data reveals that the effects of low-level, non-ionizing radiation are as harmful to human health as is exposure to ionizing radiation (from X-rays or nuclear accidents). The low-level sources include, but are not limited to: cellular telephones, video display terminals, television and radio towers, high voltage electric lines, satellites, police radios, paging systems, microwave ovens and electric games, computer screens, and electric garage-door openers.

Becoming informed about this reality makes many people feel helpless. Fortunately, there exists a practical, economical, and personally empowering approach to radiation pollution. Certain foods enhance one's resilience to radiation. In some cases, they actually detoxify the body of radioactive elements. Favoring such foods is a pre-emptive health measure.

Steven R. Schechter, N. D., in *Fighting Radiation with Foods, Herbs and Vitamins* (East West Health Books, 1988) and Sara Shannon in *Diet for an Atomic Age* (Avery Books, 1987) substantiate how "radioprotective" foods guard against low and high levels of radiation. It is not surprising that whole grains are key dietary staples in this realm.

The factors related to the radioprotective effects of whole grains—including quinoa—are:

- Grains are low in fat.
- Grains contain no cholesterol.
- Grains contain the radioprotective vitamin B_6 which helps protect the thymus gland.
- Grains are low on the food chain and so (even if exposed to radiation) do not concentrate contaminants as do foods high on the food chain (meat, dairy products, eggs and large fish).
- Grain fiber and phytates bind with radioactive substances and help the body remove the toxins.
- The bulking factor of grains lessens the intestinal transit time and so hastens the elimination of all toxins.
- Grains are neither very acid nor very alkaline, and so help us maintain a middle-range pH that increases our resistance to radiation.
- The calcium in grain helps guard against uptake of radioactive strontium.
- The vitamin E and selenium in grain helps prevent cellular damage caused by free radicals. (Free radicals are implicated in the aging process and degenerative diseases.)

The Ultimate Performance Food: The Tarahumara Indians of Mexico have a 2,000-year history as endurance athletes. An 80-mile hike is an average workout. Their diet is corn-based, meaning over half of their calories come from corn.[4]

For athletes, the complex carbohydrates found in whole grains, supplemented with dried legumes and fresh vegetables, are the ultimate fuel. While a calorie is a calorie when it comes to adding weight, a calorie is not a calorie when it comes to powering the body. "Studies dealing with various mixes or ratios of foods have repeatedly demonstrated that muscles run better and longer on the chains of energy created by (complex) carbohydrates."[5]

Whole grains contain over 70 percent complex carbohydrates, which give a steady supply of energy. The burning of these carbohydrates gives predictable and steady performance rather than the up-and-down energy swings that come from eating refined carbohydrates.

Whole-grain carbohydrates are the best substance for refueling the body's glycogen stores. Studies comparing runners eating a high-sugar diet versus a high complex-carbohydrate diet reveal that 48 hours following exercise those eating complex carbohydrates had higher glycogen stores.[6] Additionally, grains are low in fat and contain virtually all the essential nutrients needed for all-around fitness training.

Many athletes who once downed pre-game steak dinners are switching to pasta. Athletes-in-the-know specify whole grains or whole grain pasta.

Grains and Spirituality: If you are sensitive to foods, you become aware of how different foods affect your whole being. Specific foods may positively or negatively affect your mental focus, attitude, and physical performance. Scientists researching the nutrients which affect brain function note that protein can increase your mental acuity and carbohydrates can calm frazzled nerves.[7] This applies to all of us. However, food-sensitive people are generally more apt to notice it. They may include athletes, yogis, ascetics, singers, people with food allergies, chronically ill persons, vegetarians, nutritionists, and hyperactive children and their parents.

There is a significant body of experience and literature suggesting that abstinence from, or reduction of, meat may help incline one towards contemplative pursuits as opposed to worldly pursuits. The unstated corollary to meat reduction is an increase in grain intake. This is the only practical course of action as other vegetable foods lack adequate nutrients to serve as daily staples.

Yes, fruitarian, and live-food diets are exceptions. These regimes do not use grains as daily staples. They have limited historical precedents, few proponents, and are not likely to appeal to a general population. They are prescribed for a cleansing, rather than a maintenance, diet.

Various religious teachers have described the path to spiritual awakening as becoming more accessible after eliminating flesh foods from the diet. The Hindu scriptures observe that vegetable and grain foods enable one to live with a "mind pure and calm," whereas other foods excite passion, make the mind restless, unsteady and uncontrollable, lower the consciousness and increase depression, inertia and disease. Meat eating tends to stimulate one's physical passion.[8]

Mardi Gras, ("Fat Tuesday" in French) is the last day to consume meat before the 40-day fast preceding Easter. Among some orthodox Christians there is an additional 40-day fast from all animal foods prior to Christmas. This fasting is understood to encourage introspection and spiritual development. Possibly the infamous prison fare of "bread and water" was intended to incline the inmate towards self-reflection and repentance.

The trend towards holistic health and whole foods gives a new twist to diet and spirituality. If spirituality entails being a fully developed, whole, intact human being, then the consumption of whole foods contributes to one's completeness. Annemarie Colbin, head of New York City's famed Natural Gourmet Cooking School, discusses wholeness and grains in her latest book, *Food and Healing:*

> Grain consumption also has certain nonphysical, psychological or spiritual effects . . . whole grains—not cracked, or ground, but unbroken—can foster a holistic worldview. Ancient Central American Indian lore has it that grains facilitate socialization and social intercourse; and in the West, breaking bread with one's neighbor is the ultimate symbol of a spiritually strong social connection. Time and again I hear from my students that a change of diet toward one that includes a significant proportion of . . . (whole grains) has helped dramatically in changing their perception of life—from a fragmented, alienated, self-centered view to one of connection, integration, and oneness.[9]

Likewise, the consumption of partial foods contributes to one's "disintegration." Sport psychologist for the New York Mets and author Saul Miller points out:

> Within every plant or animal, there is a dynamic balance of energy. Removing or separating out the parts disturbs energy flow and balance and destroys the natural vitality of the substance. Eating unwhole foods, those that have been refined or disintegrated, appears to affect us in the same way. The foods most affected are those most frequently refined—the carbohydrates, especially grains and sugars. Since our "daily bread" is now disintegrated, it should come as no surprise that symptoms of physical and mental disintegration are widespread.[10]

This information is not a claim that spiritual development depends upon diet. Such a statement would be blatantly absurd. The development of one's relationship with spirit is an individual and personal experience which involves the totality of one's being. Diet may, or may not, have a role in such an unfolding.

Nevertheless, we have ample tradition, experience and even current scientific observation that the consumption of grains contributes to—at the least—a calm and reflective mentality. Such a mind includes an imagining of universal concerns. This perspective is historically considered conducive to developing one's spirituality. An additional, observation is that emphasis on whole foods—as opposed to refined foods—supports wholeness of body, mind and spirit.

3. Quinoa the Supergrain

Of all the whole grains, quinoa is the most nutritious and best combines versatility and speedy preparation. The only other whole grains which cook as quickly are buckwheat and teff. Quinoa is more versatile than brown rice and takes much less time to cook. As a multipurpose flour, quinoa is second only to wheat. Unlike wheat, it can be enjoyed cooked as a whole grain. It also cooks in less time and is more adaptable than millet, barley, rye, and oats. Quinoa can be used in more ways than the two other "new" grains, amaranth and teff. These features alone qualify quinoa as a *supergrain*—but we are just warming up.

Ecological Diversity and Global Health: Today most of the calories consumed throughout the world come from only seven food families. Many other foods exist, and historically humankind relied on a much wider selection of food. Two food families afford well over half of the world's food volume. They are:

- Grasses—cereal grains, bamboo and sugar cane
- Legumes—peas, beans, lentils and peanuts

The importance of the other most-used food families varies according to climatic region.

- Palms—coconut and palm kernel oil
- Cabbage family—cabbage, broccoli, Chinese cabbage, radishes and many more of our common vegetables
- Nightshades—potatoes, tomatoes and peppers
- Rose family—temperate tree fruits and some berries
- Carrot family—carrots, celery and parsnips

A few other food families like citrus, fungus, olives, grapes, sweet potatoes and seaweed figure strongly in various areas of the world.[11] Dependency upon such a few food families is a precarious situtaion. An early spokesmen for food crop diversification, Noel D. Vietmeyer of the National Research Council, says that:

> Although more than 20,000 edible plants are known, and perhaps 3,000 have been used by mankind throughout history, a mere handful of crops now dominate the world's food supply. This is a dangerously small larder from which to feed a whole planet.[12]

The problem is compounded because only a few varieties of a given food are commercially valuable. For example, the world's most abundant crop is wheat. There are tens of thousands of wheat varieties. However, only five have commercial importance in the United States. Such dependence upon an "elite" cultivar crop is dangerous, as two examples from recent history demonstrate. The mid-1800s potato crop in Ireland and the 1970s midwestern United States corn crop were each monocultures. Blight devastated both crops.

Such loss does not occur in an environment with diversified crops. In a traditional agricultural setting, for example, blight might destroy one field of corn. However, different strains of corn growing in nearby fields might be untouched. Until recent history, the foods sustaining humankind were diversified, heirloom crops, generally composed of open-pollinated and regionally adapted varieties. Today they tend to be hybridized or genetically engineered.

An important way to support ecological diversity in these times of dwindling genetic resources is to broaden our culinary tastes. Enjoying new and different foods, such as quinoa, has global impact. In practice, however, few people change their eating habits for philosophical reasons or ecological principles. Most of us consider dietary change only if it hits closer to home, specifically affecting our own health and survival.

Dr. Hugh D. Wilson, biologist at Texas A&M University who specializes in heirloom crops, observes:

> Evolutionary success requires an ability to change with changing circumstances. Narrow specialization works well only when conditions are stable. Since conditions are rarely stable, those with a broad range of available options usually survive. The agricultural system that has supported human development over the past 15,000 years was originally composed of diverse elements. (The current) simplified biological foundation . . . is indeed a critical problem.[13]

Historically those peoples and individuals who are the most resilient and flexible are most apt to survive. Eating a wide range of whole foods contributes to mental and physical resilience according to current nutritionists and holistic health-care practitioners.

Possibly we can go an additional step and include an even wider range of foods than those from the most common food families. The ancient foodstuffs may enhance our well-being by supporting our mental and physical flexibility.

Food Allergies and Quinoa: An ever-increasing number of people suffer from food allergies. One of the most common allergens is to grains from the grass family, especially wheat and corn. The leafy grains (quinoa, amaranth and buckwheat) belong to different botanical families. They are not usually allergens.* Some who suffer from allergies describe the most versatile of the leafy grains, quinoa, as a godsend for it permits a more normal diet. For example, there are now several domestic quinoa pastas available on the market. At least one variety is wheat-free for those with gluten allergies.

---

* Of hundreds of thousands of North Americans who enjoy quinoa, some may have an allergic reaction to it. I know of two instances. In one case the quinoa was washed, in the other it was unwashed and thus the reaction might have been saponin-related. Occasionally people report that daily consumption of multiple servings of unwashed quinoa may cause diarrhea.

Quinoa's Nutritional Profile: As I am writing this nutritional section, I have spread over my desk quinoa data from nine countries, seven United States universities, three domestic scientific laboratories, the National Academy of Sciences, and the United Nations Food and Agriculture Organization.

One would hope that the data concurs. It does not. Quinoa does not lend itself to tidy categorization. The nutritive data for common grains, unlike that for quinoa, is well established. They have been thoroughly scrutinized and the seeds themselves are actually patented.

Quinoa's nutritive data is not consistent because:

- Thousands of quinoa varieties are being grown today in the Andes; and several hundred are being grown elsewhere in the world. Each variety has a different nutrient profile.
- Quinoa is covered with a bitter tasting substance called saponin. Saponin removal techniques are not standardized, thus an identical seed cleaned by two different methods may produce two different nutrient data profiles.
- As with any food, nutrients depend upon soil quality, growing conditions and maturity at harvest time. Two identical varieties of any plant grown on two different plots can have two different nutritional profiles.

Despite the problems in determining quinoa's exact nutritional profile, there is still much that can be said about this grain. The available data indicates that quinoa ranges from 7.5 to 22.1 percent protein. Of common grains, hard spring wheat is the highest in protein at 14 percent. Rye, millet and brown rice are the next highest protein cereals with 12, 9, and 7.5 percent protein respectively. Thus quinoa can have "up to 50 percent more protein than other grains and is an adequate substitute for meat in a vegetarian diet."[14]

Unlike any of the grass-family grains, quinoa's protein possesses an exceptionally attractive amino acid balance for human nutrition. It has high levels of the amino acid, lysine, in which the common grains are deficient. The United Nations' Food and Agriculture Organization observes that quinoa is closer to the ideal protein balance than any other common grain, being at least equal to milk in protein quality. While no single food can supply all of the essential life-sustaining nutrients, quinoa comes as close as any other in the vegetable or animal kingdom.[15] This Andean "mother grain" has higher levels of fat, calcium, phosphorus, iron and the B-vitamins than wheat, corn, oats, or rice.[16]

A plant's regenerative essence is contained in the germ, or embryo. This is the most nutrient-rich portion of the whole plant. Relative to other grains, quinoa has an enormous embryo, and this helps explain its status as a supergrain. The germs of corn, rice and wheat are but a speck at the tip of the grain. Quinoa's germ embraces its entire circumference.

Quinoa's large germ accounts for its high protein content and helps assure its survival in harsh and adverse growing conditions. This nutrient profile may also make it useful as a human survival food. Dr. Duane Johnson, the New Crops Agronomist at Colorado State University, has been widely quoted: "If I had to choose one food to survive on, quinoa would be the best."

Nutritional Content: Quinoa is remarkably high in B-vitamins, iron, zinc, and protein. Its thiamine (B_1) content is even higher than that of chicken liver which is commonly considered the superior vitamin B_1 source. This information is for an Equadorian quinoa variety which is widely distributed in the United States. It is taken from a December 1987 analysis by Hazleton Laboratories.

Two ounces dry (approximately 1/2 cup cooked) quinoa yield:

Calories	218
Carbohydrates	37.9 g
Sodium	less than 30 mg/per 100 g
Cholesterol	less than 1 mg/per 100 g
Potassium	269 mg
Fat	3.9 g
Protein	7.8 g

	%USDRA
Protein	12.12
Thiamine	26.46
Riboflavin	10.00
Niacin	2.72
Calcium	2.48
Iron	15.84
Pyridoxine HCL (B_6)	13.61
Phosphorus	23.25
Vitamine E	6.31
Vitamin B_{12}	—
Zinc	8.32
Vitamin A	—
Vitamin C	—

Amino Acid	mg/g
Aspartic acid	12.5
Threonine	5.24
Serine	6.37
Glutamic Acid	20.6
Proline	6.19
Glycine	8.27
Alanine	6.21
Cystine	1.39
Valine	6.29
Methionine	1.68
Isoleucine	5.13
Leucine	9.03
Tyrosine	3.82
Phenylalanine	5.74
Histidine	4.96
Lysine	8.43

Ash content per 100 grams is 2.0 grams.

Quinoa's Subtle Properties: Imagine three bowls holding cooked grain. One contains white rice, another contains brown rice and the third contains quinoa. Each grain is similar in volume and has precisely the same number of calories. Now imagine eating each. Which one is the most energizing?

A nutritionist measures energy in units called calories. Today's health-aware people also categorize food by its integrity. The more refined a food is the more demand it places on the pancreas for regulation of blood sugar. Also, the more it stresses the immune system. Brown rice rates better than does white rice. White rice has more vitality than white rice flour.

It is reasonable to hypothesize that quinoa, which grows in a rigorous environment and is less cultivated, hybridized, and civilized than brown rice, should impart more vital energy than does brown rice. Certainly, anecdotal evidence suggests that it does.

The stamina of quinoa-eating populations illustrates this well. In 1974, the Welsh adventurer, sailor, and author, Tristan Jones, spent seven months sailing on the Andean Lake Titicaca (elevation 12,850 feet). He was the first to chart the lake. In *The Incredible Voyage* Jones recounts:

> I had often seen . . . the Indians standing in the freezing waters of the Lake, fishing for hours on end, when I could barely keep my hand in the same water for more than a minute . . . the Andes Indians surpass any other race I've ever been in contact with, including the Eskimos, for hardiness.[17]

Quinoa and Holistic Health: The holistic view of health is gaining increasing acceptance. It recognizes that our environment and diet affect our physical, emotional, and spiritual well-being. It maintains that survival depends upon how well one harmonizes with one's ecosystem. Quinoa's amazing survival skills in difficult conditions may help those who eat quinoa adapt to unhealthful environmental conditions.

This goosefoot plant has minute vessels (*vesiculate pubescence*) on its leaves which contain calcium oxalate crystals that protect the plant from high irradiation.[18] Natural solar radiation at high elevations is intense because the thin air offers far less protection than does the more dense air of lower elevations. On hot dry days at high elevations, the quinoa leaves retain their moisture because of their calcium oxalate crystals. Other plants become dehydrated and, if not watered, they perish.

During the disastrous Bolivian drought of 1982 and 1983, quinoa thrived while over 50 percent of the potato and barley crop was lost and nearly half of the vegetable, fruit, and wheat crop was devastated. Drought damage is intensified in areas of high solar radiation, but quinoa has so adapted that in the same drought period in Peru "drier-than-normal weather even produced bumper yields of quinoa."[19]

Quinoa as Medicine: A 1758 Spanish travel journal describes quinoa as being like rice and "has a very pleasant taste" and that the cooking water is used as an "apozem" (soothing infusion). For external applications it is ground, boiled and applied to the part affected, from which it soon extracts all corrupt humors occasioned by a contusion.[20]

Other historical literature notes that quinoa and cañihua were used as diuretics and emetics. They were also considered effective in the treatment of liver problems, urinary disorders, tuberculosis, cholera, appendicitis and cancer. The two chenopods were also used for motion sickness and *soroche* (altitude sickness).[21]

While in the Andes I asked diverse people about the medicinal properties of quinoa. Included in my informal poll were nutritionists, foreign-aid professionals, agronomists, shamans, herbalists, and *campesinos* (country people). The answers, which repeated themselves, were that quinoa is good for altitude sickness and bone problems (its high calcium content supports this). A common claim is that quinoa strengthens mother's milk and is strengthening for pregnancy and the postpartum period. Black quinoa varieties are said to be good for tuberculosis and the digestive system.

Typical non-professional advice for broken bones was to eat quinoa and to use it as an external plaster. Plasters are made of quinoa flour mixed with water or egg. Such a poultice is also used for drawing out infections.

In the Cuzco Indian market, a Quechua friend, Narcisco Cicahuana, introduced me to one of the respected Callawaya Indians. For centuries, the Callawayas have traveled throughout the altiplano practicing their ancient herbal arts. Most *campesinos* prefer these herbalists over doctors. Their pharmacopoeia includes a vast array of dried bark, seeds, flowers, and animal parts. They also work with brightly colored aluminum amulets.

The Callawaya herbalist gently and softly greeted us. We shared an orange soda and then talked. I told him of my interest in the medicinal properties of quinoa. With an inch-wide sea shell he scooped a few measures of a specialty quinoa into a scrap of paper, carefully folded the paper and presented it to me. He said,

> Quinoa is medicine for soul calling. When a person's soul is out or has sunk into the ground give him a massage with quinoa and then bury the grain on the spot where the problem first manifest.

Perhaps more relevant to modern man is quinoa's potential as a radioprotective food. As noted in the preceding chapter, grains are an optimum radioprotective food because of their nutritive profile. Quinoa has a higher ash (mineral) and B-vitamin content than the common grains, which suggests that as a radioprotective food it is even superior to them. Vitamin B_6 is considered the most radioprotective vitamin. A two-ounce serving of quinoa provides a whopping 14 percent of the USDRA for B_6.

Endurance Food: Because they are high in carbohydrates, low in fat, and rich in vitamins and minerals, whole grains enhance physical endurance (see preceding chapter). It is reasonable to assume that since quinoa has a superior nutritional profile to other grains it provides greater endurance. But quinoa may do even more than this.

Life forms adapt to their specific environment. Nearly every one of the altiplano major food plants contains substances toxic to people but which allow it to survive the extreme environment. By 1000 B.C. the proto-Aymaras (the ancestors of the current Aymara peoples) had developed detoxification techniques for their food plants. Nontoxic mutations were also isolated and propagated. Their unique cultivars were adapted to survive in the harsh environment and to sustain those who cultivated them.[22]

The average elevation of Bolivia is over 12,000 feet. Tourists often experience lethargy and flu-like symptoms because of the reduced oxygen supply. At 17,000 feet there is not enough oxygen for normal metabolism of amino acids. Contemporary climbers may experience muscle deterioration which becomes progressively more rapid the higher they climb. Today oxygen masks are standard gear for climbers at 20,000 feet and above.

In Incan times, sandal-clad workers built lookouts, courtyards and altars on peaks above 20,000 feet. At one such summit, a rock-wall courtyard had been leveled with nearly 100 tons of earth backpacked from below.[23] These people were, and are, remarkably adapted to the high altitude.

During Incan times corps of *chasquis* or post runners relayed news throughout the empire, which spanned 2,500 miles and was similar in size to the Roman Empire. This domain contained slopes rising four vertical miles and ranging from tropical to polar climates. Relay teams of the barefoot *chasquìs* covered about 150 miles in a 24-hour period, which could involve running full speed on moonless nights.[24]

Today sports trainers and historians attribute the prowess of the *chasquis* to their use of coca leaves. Coca leaf, from which cocaine is derived, is used to enhance oxygen availability. (Coca leaf is also an appetite depressant and a slight hallucinogen.) A few coca leaves and the ash of the quinoa plant are tucked into the cheek and held there like a chew of tobacco. The quinoa ash releases alkaloids in the coca which enable the red blood cells to carry more oxygen. This practice remains widespread throughout the altiplano today. If you look closely at the Indians (or photographs of them) you often see a characteristic bulge in their cheeks.

It is possible that the Indians' ability to function at high altitudes is due to more than coca. Coca was not forgotten by Western civilization, and its properties are well documented. Quinoa, the nearly forgotten food, lacks comparable documentation. There are ample circumstantial evidence and historical accounts, however, to warrant quinoa's serious consideration as a high endurance food for low oxygen availability sports.

Two friends of mine, Andre and Jyoti Ulrich, have some experience with quinoa at high elevations. They participated in the Americans to China Expedition in 1986, which included ascending the west ridge of Mt. Everest. The Ulrichs, who happen to grow quinoa in their Aspen, Colorado home garden, also enjoy eating it. Quinoa was one of their food staples while on the trek. Andre, age 52, reported to me:

> For four days I was at 25,000 feet and I felt great and had plenty of energy. I fared much better than many of our group who were much younger. I attribute this to my diet and life style. Twelve years ago I reached 25,000 feet on Makalu [the third highest Himalayan peak]. At that time I was not eating a grain-based diet and I suffered intensely from altitude sickness.

Quinoa and Spirituality: There is some popular sentiment that quinoa enhances one's psychic and/or spiritual development. In the previous chapter, we examined the evidence that grain consumption supports meditative activities. Let us review what little evidence there is specifically for quinoa.

According to Dr. Ismael Escobar, nuclear physicist at a 17,000-foot cosmic ray laboratory near La Paz, Bolivia, at high elevations there is less atmospheric shielding and so ". . . there are sharper extremes of light and shadow, heat and cold, day and night. And the impact of galactic gamma rays is easier to detect."[25]

The atmospheric pressure is significantly less than at sea level. This extreme environment enables those living in, or visiting the area, to experience unusual sensory perceptions. Possibly this becomes translated as paranormal experience.

One person who has popularized psychic phenomena is actress/author Shirley MacLaine. Miss MacLaine's T.V. miniseries described her psychic experiences in Peru. MacLaine's account helped increase the existing aura of magic and spiritualism already surrounding the altiplano people and their country. Some extend this association to their food staple.

The association of quinoa with spirituality may also be attributed to a Bolivian named

Jyoti Ulrich and quinoa on Mt. Everest (page 39)

Oscar Ichazo. Ichazo created a spiritual organization, Arica Institute, that had several thousand members in the United States in the 1970s. Ichazo informed his students that quinoa consumption helped develop sensitivity during meditation. The only problem for Arica students was that quinoa was not available in the United States. Years later two of Ichazo's students, Stephen Gorad and Don McKinley, initiated its successful introduction into the United States market.

From another quarter comes support that quinoa helps one's inner development. Many people throughout the world favor heirloom seed crops because they are self-sustainable. (Hybrid and genetically engineered seeds do not reproduce true.) People who favor ancient food crops observe that non-hybrid seeds impart the greatest vitality. This information also contributes to quinoa's reputation as supergrain which supports total health.

The above information certainly does not present a tight case for quinoa as food which promotes spiritual or psychic development. It may, however, suggest to some, grounds for personal experimentation.

4. Corn the Upstart—Goosefoot in Prehistoric North America

This chapter contains two stories. One is a mystery and needs a good sleuth. The other story is about creation, and it invites you to re-create. In a roundabout way, both bring the quinoa story into your own backyard.

Corn is considered North America's native grain, but corn is an upstart. As a staple, Indians in the eastern United States had relied on it only for a scant 500 years before the Mayflower landed. Corn was introduced from Central America into the Eastern Woodlands earlier, around A.D. 350, but its use was marginal. Stable carbon isotope studies indicate that maize did not become a major dietary component of these early northern populations until about A.D. 1150; this was concurrent with a diminishing of chenopods.[26]

The actual traditional North American grain has a 5,000-year history. A near-sister to quinoa, it is a goosefoot (*Chenopodium berlandieri* ssp. *jonesianum*). There are numerous historical references to various peoples throughout North America foraging goosefoot leaves and seed. Anthropologist Ruth Underhill quotes a Papago Indian from southern Arizona who recalled their use:

> We always kept gruel in our house. It was in a big clay pot that my mother had made. She ground up seeds into flour. Not wheat flour—we had no wheat. But all the wild seeds, the good pigweed [goosefoot] and the wild grasses . . . Oh, good that gruel was! I have never tasted anything like it. Wheat flour makes me sick. I think it has no strength. But when I am weak, when I am tired, my grandchildren make me a gruel out of wild seeds. That is *food.*[27]

Historical records of goosefoot as a cultivated crop are scant. One is a 1750 account by a French adventurer DuPratz and the Natchez Indians who scattered *belle dame sauvage* (the French name for a common chenopod) on the sandy banks of the Mississippi River and kicked sand over them:

> . . . after this sowing and this kind of cultivation they wait until autumn, and then gather a great quantity of this grain. They prepare it like millet and it is very good eating.[28]

Our contemporary names for the weedy relatives of the ancient cultivated chenopods are goosefoot, lamb's-quarters and pigweed. History lacks records for the historic names of the indigenous crop. Two popular chenopods foraged in Britain are fat hen and Good King Henry. The greens of various goosefoot plants, primarily foraged, figure in cuisines throughout the world. The domestication of chenopods for use as seed plants is apparently limited to the Americas.

There is abundant archeobotanical evidence of the goosefoot as a major food crop in the eastern United States. Seeds have been found in archeological sites in Alabama, Arkansas, Illinois, Iowa, Kentucky, Louisiana, Michigan, Missouri, Nebraska, New York, Ohio, Pennsylvania and Tennessee.[29]

One such finding was at the Russell Cave in northeastern Alabama. In 1961 scientists recovered the charred remains of a small basket containing 49,650 *Chenopodium* seeds. The Smithsonian Institution Radiocarbon Laboratory dated the age of the basket and seeds at 1975 B.C. "Ninety-two percent of the analyzed fruits exhibited the distinctive . . . characteristic(s) of domesticated varieties of *Chenopodium*."[30]

When corn became the dominant food around 800 years ago in the Eastern Woodlands region of what is now the United States, the chenopod was still grown, but its importance decreased. This was in direct contrast to the Andes and Mexico, where the leafy grains, quinoa and amaranth, remained the primary staples and the key religious grains, despite the prevalence of the grass-family grain, maize.

Today, amaranth is commonly regarded as the sacred grain of the Aztec. One of America's leading authorities on ancient Mexican cultivars, Hugh D. Wilson, Ph.D., of Texas A&M University, suggests that chenopods, along with amaranth, were also considered sacred by the Aztec. According to a 1519 report:

> "a dicotyledonous 'pseudocereal' called 'huauthli' or 'guautli' (huauzontle is the contemporary name of the cultivated goosefoot) . . . played a significant role in Mexican religious activity, including ceremonial human sacrifice."[31]

Religious significance notwithstanding, there is ample archeological evidence that the Aztec domesticated a chenopod as well as amaranth. These two grains were similar in size and use and were three times more abundant than corn at the time of Cortez according to Dr. Wilson.

Starting with the European invasion of the Americas in the 1500s there was cultural destruction, population decline, and religious suppression of native populations. The Spanish actively prevented cultivation of the sacred grains in both Central and South America. However, they saw the economic potential of the New World crops maize, sunflower, squash and nightshades (potatoes, peppers and tomatoes). These less sacred foods were soon growing throughout the world.

What Happened to the Valued Goosefoot? Here is the unsolved mystery. Why was the original staple grain of what is now the eastern United States "lost?" Why did these indigenous peoples, unlike many other tribes throughout the Americas, eventually favor corn cultivation? Why did European settlers in northeastern America fail to see the value of goosefoot while capitalizing on other native cultivars?

There is no evidence or suggestion that the Pilgrims actively suppressed goosefoot agriculture. Because of its similarity to their "weeds" back home, did they assume it had no commercial value? Because of goosefoot's small seed size was it considered less valuable than corn? We can only hypothesize.

Another mystery about the North American cultivated chenopod is its origin. Some experts maintain that it was originally domesticated in Mexico and traded into the Eastern Woodlands region. Others maintain that goosefoot was independently domesticated in both areas. (See *Bibliography* for further reading.)

***Chenopodium* seed heads.**

Sample B is a 4000-year-old fragment from an Ozark Bluff Dweller site in Arkansas. It, and the contemporary plant (A), show compact seed heads typical of domestication. The contemporary lamb's-quarters (C) has numerous small clusters of seeds typical of a wild goosefoot plant. (Photo courtesy of Hugh D. Wilson.)

Re-Creation: In your own backyard, you may easily start changing a weedy goosefoot into a cultivar. It is unlikely that such an exercise would have commercial value, but imagine the sheer wonder of it all! First, let us see how the process has already happened once.

Archeobotanist Bruce D. Smith, of the Smithsonian Institution, maps the domestication of eastern North American seed crops, including the chenopods, in great detail. Here is a distillation of his sketch: Early humans were very mobile and foraged their staple foods. During the period of 8000 B.C. to 4000 B.C. climatic changes supported the development of permanent year-round settlements. The people became harvesters.

With established homes, the ground surface around the settlements became disturbed from building sites, refuse dumps, and pathways. When foraged seeds were brought home for processing, storage and consumption, some of the seeds were "lost" into the surrounding disturbed soil and grew. These initially were unmanaged weed-gardens.

By 3500 B.C. humans differentiated between "crops" and "weeds," and started to actively husband the food plants. In time, what initially had been wild plants became more dependable, more easily monitored and more abundant food sources.

As this process continued over millennia, the seeds themselves changed. The most vigorous seedlings and those which sprouted first were more apt to survive and provide seed for the following year. Likewise, those plants with the largest seed heads were most easily harvested. Another beneficial plant characteristic was delayed shattering. Those seeds which ripened and dispersed from the plant earlier than the majority of the seeds were unlikely to be harvested. Early maturing seeds probably did not contribute to the gene pool for succeeding crops.[32]

These morphological changes which made chenopodium a cultivated grain insured its demise when people stopped gardening it. A cultivated crop loses its ability to survive in the wild. Consequently, the oldest grain staple of North America, the goosefoot, is extinct as an agricultural crop. Some of its gene pool survives due to its hybridization with the chenopod weed, lamb's-quarters. The Mexican chenopod crops, *chia*,* *huauzontle* and *quelite* are also related.

Now, it is your turn. Find a patch of lamb's-quarters. This is an easy task even in urban areas. As ubiquitous as dandelions, they favor empty lots, unkempt gardens, roadsides and abandoned fields. Lamb's-quarters leaves are whitish-green and appear as if they were sprinkled with white powder. The leaves range from almost an inch to two-inches long and have the three-lobed, characteristic goosefoot shape. The stems range from one to five feet tall. As the plant matures, the stem base becomes streaked with reddish-purple. The inconspicuous flowers are without petals.

Your act of creation is going to be relatively easy. Of the plant realm, the genus *Chenopodium* is considered easy to domesticate because it is such a resilient, hardy plant and grows under a wide variety of cultural conditions. Lamb's-quarters are weedy in nature and so are already leaning toward domestication.

Visit your weed patch throughout the growing season. If it is in an environmentally clean area, harvest some of the top, tender young greens throughout spring and early summer. They are delicious in a salad (see recipe page 108) or when prepared like spinach. When seeds are ripe and dry, return to the plant with a paper bag or plastic

* Chia also refers to seeds of salvia species.

sack. Bend the seed head into the bag. Grasp the stalk with one hand and, in a downward motion, strip the seeds (and leaves) into the bag. Sift out the plant debris (see page 177).

In a good lamb's-quarters stand you can easily harvest several cups of seed in as many minutes. If you have a vivid imagination, foraging for wild seed is apt to trigger wild fantasies. In addition, you will have a free supply of nature's bounty to add to soups and grain dishes.

Starting with a wild population of goosefoot, you can create an improved strain. At harvest time, scatter some wild seed in a corner of your garden. Next year harvest this crop and reserve seed from the plants which have the most desirable characteristics. Sow this selected seed. Repeat annually.

Within ten to fifteen years of selection, your goosefoot will exhibit morphological changes. It will take longer to develop a vital cultivar with a large seed head, thin outer shell, and delayed shattering mechanism. Leave instructions in your will to repeat this process for a millenium. There, in a manner of speaking, you would approximate the re-creation of the North American quinoa-like grain.

Quinoa field, Crestone, Colorado

5. Quinoa in South America—Prehistory Through Spanish Conquest

The kullku (turtle dove) brought three seeds to the people. The seeds were planted and became quinoa, cañihua and kiwicha.—*Quechua myth*

According to popular mythology, the altiplano grains were heavenly gifts delivered by a sacred bird. Of these grains, quinoa was, and is, the most important. As food staples, cañihua and kiwicha (a chenopod and an amaranth respectively) were and are less important. Their very small size limits their appeal to the United States consumer. Cañihua is noteworthy, however, for it survives even lower temperatures than does quinoa.

Taxonomists observe that the bulk of all plants originated in key floristic regions. Each of these regions has great environmental extremes. Of the world's floristic regions, one of the most ecologically diversified is the Andean altiplano.

The Andes are a rugged young mountain range with glacier-filled high valleys. In these high mountain plateaus of Peru, Bolivia, and parts of Ecuador and Chile, it rains during spring, but the other nine months are dry. Due to decreased atmospheric pressure, there is forty percent less oxygen than at sea level. When it freezes no frost forms because the air is so thin and dry. A precipitous four-mile descent brings one into tropical rain forests. Here in the altiplano humankind lives in more extreme conditions than anywhere else in the world.

The altiplano is a small geographical area relative to all of South America. But its impact on the whole continent is major. According to the renowned taxonomist, N. I. Vavilov, it is "apparent that both plant and animal husbandry in South America had its start in the puno (altiplano)."[33]

To sustain life in this harsh environment, the Indians developed unique domesticated animals (such as the llama and alpaca) and crops. Of the plants, quinoa is indeed remarkable. It will set seed and mature when receiving as little as three-and-a-half inches of precipitation and when exposed to below freezing temperatures.[34] However, in such adverse conditions, yields are low. That quinoa produces at all in such severe circumstances is significant to those whose very lives depend upon their harvest. In the southern altiplano quinoa is the monocrop and typically receives ten inches of precipitation in non-drought years. The farming conditions to the north are less harsh.

Archeobotanists have sifted through the debris of ancient villages to piece together the story of quinoa cultivation. Eight or nine millennia ago in the Lake Titicaca region, the Indians started transforming quinoa from a wild plant to a cultivated crop. Between 5,000 and 7,000 years ago, the seed showed the morphological characteristics of a grain.

These signs include a larger-sized fruit, a thin shell, and non-shattering inflorescences. Apparently, at the same time and in the same way, chenopod domestication also occurred in Mesoamerica and the northeastern American woodlands (see Chapter 4).*

By 1000 B.C. the early Aymara people living in the altiplano had diets and lifestyles relatively the same as their contemporary descendants living in isolated hamlets today. Quinoa was the grain staple, and still is.

Dr. David L. Browman is an Andean archeologist specializing in the origins of domesticated plants and animals. He and his research staff at Washington University in St. Louis have excavated five different time periods of an early (pre-600 B.C. to A.D. 500) farming village at Chiripa, Bolivia. This lakeshore site is located on the southwest corner of Lake Titicaca, on the Taraco peninsula.

Dr. Browman's research reveals that quinoa was the staple grain. "Chenopodium seeds were the most important component of the seed remains recovered, constituting from seventy to ninety percent of the materials."[35] Given the central role of quinoa in the diet, it is not surprising that its Aymara name *la chisiya mama* means mother grain.**

Around the time of the Roman Empire the Huarpa Indian culture had developed sophisticated irrigation systems and terraces of *andenes*. They lived in the Ayacucho desert region which is south of La Paz. The Huarpas so successfully used the scant rainfall that five times more land was then agriculturally productive than is today. The Huarpa terraces are carefully built rock walls. Centuries later the Incas made similar looking terraces.[37]

Farming in much of the altiplano was, and is, an up-down activity rather than a horizontal one. Often a farmer's upper terrace is 2,000 feet higher than his lower terrace. The andenes enabled successful farming and prevented erosion on otherwise impossibly steep slopes. On gradual inclines, the terraces are twelve feet or more wide. On more vertical inclines andenes are as narrow as six inches.

The Tiahuanaco, or Aymara, culture flourished from A.D. 100 to A.D. 1200. These people evoke fantasy. The advances of their civilization and their far-reaching impact over the whole Andean region was greater than that of the Incas.[38] Their pottery and textiles show a refined degree of skill and beauty. Their intriguing stone masonry was as advanced as their knowledge of agriculture and the movement of heavenly bodies.

The major site of the high Tiahuanaco culture is located in Bolivia between La Paz and Lake Titicaca. It was built upon the lake shore—which has since receded—and rivaled ancient Greece in its grandeur. Today Tiahuanaco is situated in a quiet farming area and its geographical surroundings are not highly photogenic (certainly not relative to the best-known Incan site, Machu Picchu). This, plus shoddy and jejune excavation attempts, contribute to its obscurity.

According to legend, the creator of the world, Viracocha, dwelt here. (Illustration on

* Some research indicates that the chenopods were domesticated independently at two American sites and then traded to other areas.

** Other Andean regional names for quinoa include: *quinua, kiuna, suba, chancas, jupa, jiura* and *pasca.*

Spanish names include: *quinua, kinoa, trigrillo, trigo inca, arroz del Peru, dahua* and *hupa.*

Portuguese names include: *arroz miudo do Peru* and *espinafre do Peru.*

French names: *anserine quinoa, riz de Peru, quinoa.*

German names: *Reisspinat, peruanischer Reisspinat* and *Reismelde.*[36]

page 49 shows Viracocha, with tears streaming down his face, as he appears in relief on the main stone portal.) To create the various tribes, Viracocha first carved human shapes in his own image. He called these first people to life and they built the Tiahuanaco temple as his residence. Viracocha then sent them forth to people the world.

When I walked among the Tiahuanaco ruins, the pottery shards formed a thick layer of debris. I sat atop the unexcavated Akapana pyramid and marveled at the elaborate courtyards below. To me the most striking features were the faces—human and non-human—protruding from massive stone walls. I wondered what these faces might have seen in their nearly 2,000 years.

In my travels throughout the Americas and Europe I have enjoyed visiting ancient sites. Each has its distinctive ambiance. At Tiahuanaco I sensed a peace and timelessness. I wondered about the people who built these walls and their strength, endurance and sophistication. I thought of how quinoa was transformed from a wild plant to a grain staple in this area. I pondered the profound connection between our souls and our soils. And I dreamed, sitting there 5,000 miles away from home, of planting next year's garden.

The Incas:

> The sun took pity on the people and sent the first Inca, Manco Capac, and his sister-wife, Mama Ocllo. This couple emerged from Lake Titicaca and, according to the sun's instructions, wandered until they came to a place where the golden taquiza (planting stick) sank into the earth with a single thrust. Manco Capac wrested this place from its inhabitants, named it Cuzco, which means "navel of the world," and built a temple to the sun. Thus started the Incan Empire.[39]

Although there are numerous variations of the first Inca's story, this one contains the most common themes. The semimythical Manco Capac established his realm sometime before A.D. 1300 and was succeeded by his male descendants. The first seven Inca rulers were content to govern their immediate valley. The eighth Inca started conquest beyond Cuzco in the early 1400s. The three following rulers created the far-reaching Incan Empire. In 1527, with the death of the eleventh Inca, the empire was torn by civil strife. Five years later, Francisco Pizarro conquered the mighty Incas with a tiny army of 158 men.

The golden taquiza given to Manco Capac by the sun was the Inca's symbol of state. One of the ruler's key functions was to study the stars and the 12-month, 360-day calendar, and to divine a propitious time to plant quinoa.[40] The Inca would ceremoniously break the first ground with his golden taquiza. The Sapa Inca (god-king) was held personally responsible for the crop's success and his people's well-being. Like the sun, the Inca's function was to shower his people with blessings. Sowing seed was a kingly act.

As with other agrarian civilizations, festivals marked key days in the agricultural cycle. At festival time Incans drank *chicha*, a beer made from fermented quinoa or maize; and offered sacrifices of children, animals, textiles and food.

The Inca turned their Bronze Age skills to create a social state in which there was little risk of real hunger. The road system and government storehouses provided food reserves in case of local shortages.[41] Other cultures at similar stages of technological development broke up into competitive states. The Incas' genius lay in their social unification. As C.A. Burland explains in, *Peru under the Inca:*

> The aim was to become a good citizen, working for the Sun, the Sapa Inca, and one's neighbors. It did not involve the separation of the individual from the community.[42]

In direct contrast to our modern society, the need for individuation is not strong in a rooted society. The Incas, with their enormous social organization and social welfare system, provide an unparalleled example of concern for the community. This quality remains strong today, especially in rural areas. To understand contemporary altiplano peoples, one must consider their rich past.

The *Conquistadores*: In one short year the Spanish obliterated the Incan civilization. One shudders to imagine the rapacity and brutality with which it was accomplished.

The retelling of that tale is not within the scope of this book—but how Spanish avarice affected quinoa is of relevance.

An efficient way to subdue a people is to take away their most cherished beliefs. The divinity of the Inca's staple food and their god-king had no place in the Catholic scheme of things. Both were eliminated. The Spanish chroniclers detailed the Sapa Inca's murder. They did not recount quinoa's demise. The results of their actions speak for themselves.

The Spanish introduced Incan corn and potatoes throughout the world, but not quinoa. The former quinoa fields and terraces soon were growing barley. This less nutritious grain was a necessary crop for the Spaniard's beer. Only in areas too remote for surveillance or too high for barley cultivation was quinoa surreptitiously grown.

What had been for thousands of years the revered food staple for millions became synonymous with dirt, illiteracy, poverty and chicken-feed. The altiplano peoples became reluctant to give their children quinoa for fear it would make them stupid. The nutritionally inferior but socially acceptable potato became the principal food. Concurrent with the loss of their grain staple came malnutrition and a pathetically high (30%) rate of infant mortality. The consequences of colonial greed still ravage the Indians.

6. Quinoa in the Altiplano Today

From the train window the Peruvian landscape unfolds before me. I am four hours south of Cuzco and headed toward Lake Titicaca. The train carries me higher into the altiplano, the cradle of quinoa cultivation. Occasional eucalyptus trees grow below the tree line and scrub brush fills the creek bottoms. Otherwise the ground volunteers nothing but tawny bunch grass and an endless variety of earth tones. The huts, people, fields, adobe walls, and hills are a study in brown. The Quechua call the earth *Pacha Mama.* My recurring impressions all have to do with earth—earth-mother, earth-children and earth-colors.

The terraces halfway up the bare, buff mountains are not yet showing green. Here at valley level the quinoa is up. Green *tarwi* (the Andean "soybean") fields with their perky purple blossoms, occasional yellow flowering weeds, and the people's bright clothing are the rare color contrasts to the earth-tones. How unlike spring hues back home in Colorado.

Utility lines faithfully follow the train tracks with never a spur to the hamlets. The tiny country buildings are one-room adobe hovels with thatched roofs and no chimneys or windows. Around these shelters I see pigs routing, roosters heckling hens, and children playing with makeshift balls and kites.

This chill, harsh land is peopled with barefoot or sandal-clad Indians who look Tibetan. As the train gains in elevation, the people become shorter and darker. Many Indians are under five feet. Their barrel-like chests attest to their increased lung and heart capacity, a necessary adaptation to thin air. The people are inseparable from the countryside. They are walking, gathering around an outdoor cookfire, weaving, tending llamas, ploughing, playing, napping, or washing clothing in the river. No one is jogging.

Bicycles and vehicles are rare in the country and are exclusively operated by males. The older men wear traditional llama wool pants and *sarapes.* Males of all ages wear *chorros,* the pointed alpaca hats with earflaps. The more urban Indians bedeck their chorros with the North American gift to world fashion, the baseball hat.

The Incas displaced over 100 tribal languages with Quechua which, along with Aymara, remain the predominant altiplano tongues. The various tribes, however, kept their grange-like community orientation and their native costume. It is five hundred years since Incan times and still a rural person's clothing precisely identifies his or her locale. The most blatant regional costume differences are the women's felt headgear. There are bowlers, derbys, helmets, miters, disks, mortarboards, and tricorners, and they run the gamut from simple to elaborate in both design and color.

The women's dramatic *Pacha Mama* costume makes them look as wide as they are tall. Their showy circular skirts are buoyed by layer upon layer of petticoats. To further accent this stocky look, the skirts are pleated horizontally and are topped with horizontally pleated aprons. Bundles are ubiquitous upon the backs of women and girls. Brightly colored handwoven alpaca *lliglla* (shawls) secure infants or goods on sturdy backs. The ends of the women's long black braids are tied together and dangle down to their waists, and their heads are inevitably crowned with their marvelously preposterous hats.

Small llama and sheep flocks range the countryside. Here a boy minds seven llamas; down the track a woman spins and watches some sheep. The few Andean beasts of burden are most often with burden. In a day's drive back home I see thousands of cattle and never a herdsman, hundreds of horses and rarely a horseman.

As were their Incan ancestors, these Indians are primarily vegetarian. The harsh landscape does not support food in abundance. It is more efficient to eat available plant foods than to use them as animal feed and then eat the animals. The potato-based diet of the poor—and poor in South America is synonymous with Indian—is occasionally supplemented with the flesh of *cuy* (guinea pigs), pigs, chicken, llama or sheep.

Since arriving in Peru a week earlier, my days have been filled with ferreting out quinoa information and visiting ancient sites and rural markets. Now this trip by train, boat, and bus to La Paz, Bolivia, allows me a chance to sit back and watch. It does not occur to me to pick up a book—the changing countryside and the beautiful people fully capture my attention.

As the train gains in altitude (and distance south of the equator) the weather becomes colder. In this November spring time the farmers are just now ploughing and sowing their fields. Trees become nonexistent. For one who does not love the earth, this stark landscape could be mistaken as ugly.

The fields are most often worked by couples. The man breaks the ground with a *chaqui taclla*, an L-shaped foot-hoe made of sticks. His seed-sowing wife follows. A few more wealthy farmers guide crude wooden ploughs pulled by oxen wearing ancient yokes. I travel hundreds of miles through cultivated land and see precisely three tractors but not a single wheelbarrow. (Urban construction sites occasionally boast wheelbarrows, but most often materials and debris are carried in arms or upon backs.)

The quinoa available on market shelves in both North and South America frequently comes from such fields. In some cases its saponin has been washed off by hand in rivers and the grain then sun-dried. There is no other commercial grain crop available in the United States which includes hand-sown, hand-weeded, hand-harvested, hand-threshed and hand-washed seed.

In Andean markets quinoa is available whole, flaked, puffed, as a flour, in *humintas* (tamales) and fermented into the beer-like *chicha*. Still, relative to wheat products, quinoa consumption is barely significant. Their current staple grains—wheat and rice—do not grow at altiplano heights. Ninety percent of Peru's wheat is imported.[43] This creates a precarious and dependent economy with hungry people although hunger was unknown in Incan times.

Imported food provides calories for a day but does not provide long-term solutions. White bread made of American-grown wheat costs less than quinoa because imported foods are subsidized. Food subsidization creates unfair competition for local food producers. Multinational businesses encourage imported-food consumption which exacerbates dependency. The Green Revolution's support of agribusiness and major world crops undermines self-sufficient small farmers and local crops. All these factors contribute to the current food crisis.*

* For further reading see *World Hunger: 10 Myths* by Frances Moore Lappé and Joseph Collins.

An altiplano counter-movement to the Green Revolution and high-yield grains was organized in the late 1960s by Mario Tapia and Humberto Gandorillos. By the mid-1970s internationally supported research groups were in Ecuador, Peru, and Bolivia promoting the use of quinoa and other indigenous crops. The hope is that quinoa's acceptance in the United States will support these national efforts in the Andean countries.

A refreshing counterpoint to the short-sighted aid programs are a new genre of self-help assistance programs which support the use of regional foods. These nonprofit organizations help teach local people how to use their own skills to improve their own economy and health. Below is one example of a self-help program in Bolivia's Comacho Province. But first some background:

Camacho borders Peru on the northeast side of Lake Titicaca and is peopled by Aymaras. Their infant death rate is over 30 percent. For every hundred births, over thirty infants will perish within their first year. A malnourished mother's milk is inadequate, so babies are weaned early to watery soup broths. The few morsels contained in the family soup pot go to those with teeth. Fuel is scarce in this treeless environment, which further intensifies hunger problems.

Potatoes, even when there are enough to go around, are an inadequate primary staple. Quinoa is the best-adapted grain for this high and arid region and every Aymara family grows some. However, it is too time-intensive a product to substantially offset hunger. A lot of seed is lost during primitive harvesting and hand threshing. Poor storage systems and laborious hand saponin removal further decreases the yield. With current farming conditions quinoa yields a pathetically small harvest of four hundred pounds per acre. On farms with efficient planting, harvesting, threshing, and saponin removal, quinoa yields up to three thousand pounds per acre.[44]

The international nonprofit organization, Freedom from Hunger Foundation (FFHF), has a pilot project in the Camacho Province. They are backed by a regional support office with Aymara-speaking people in the Bolivian capitol, La Paz. The FFHF focus is on education, nutrition, and health, and they are collaborating with other groups who have complementary skills.

Working with Solar Box Cooker, International, they have adapted an inexpensive solar pot for altiplano use. This solar crockpot is made of cardboard (or plywood), tinfoil, and a glass lid. On a sunny day it cooks quinoa in two to three hours. It is invaluable in an area where the only fuel is dung and twigs, where fires sputter for lack of oxygen, and cooking takes much longer than at sea level because of the low boiling point.

According to FFHF's Aron Zazueta, over a thousand people in Camacho are anticipating a day-long workshop. At these workshops each person will make his/her own cooker. Mr. Zazueta reports that this program will begin following the 1988 rainy season. Once in full use in Camacho, plans are to introduce solar cookers throughout the altiplano.

The cooker is one application of appropriate technology. There is also the challenge of making quinoa harvest, threshing, and saponin removal more efficient. A volunteer team of Pillsbury Company research and development scientists are working with FFHF in this area. Add the Pillsbury resources to FFHF's cultural understanding and existing on-site workers, and it is a dynamic link-up.

I met Edward L. Galle, one of the Pillsbury engineers who is adapting existing equipment for the altiplano project. Galle had equipment ready for a field test, so he scheduled his vacation to coincide with the Colorado quinoa harvest. He loaded this test machinery into a U-Haul trailer, hooked it behind the family car, and he and his wife headed out from Minneapolis.

Onto the quinoa field in Crestone, Colorado, Galle unloaded a hand-operated threshing machine and Japanese-designed rice pearler. Each is about the size of a kitchen chair. The pearler is adapted to mechanically remove quinoa saponin. Even with the conveniences of the elite—a kitchen sink and running water—it takes ten minutes to wash the saponin from a pound of quinoa. Naturally, when Aymaras wash quinoa in the stream, it takes much longer and much grain is lost to the current.

Galle's adapted pearler passed the test; it took one minute to clean one pound, and virtually none was lost. Imagine the time and seed saved if every village had one of these rice pearlers. This equipment, the solar cooker, and similar technology, are starting to effectively help nurture hungry people.

On the last leg of my South American trip, in La Paz, Bolivia, the impact of the poverty fully hit me as I saw thousands of people living in the street. Despite their impossible circumstances, the Indians maintain their dignity. They break my heart. And they inspire me.

Also inspiring is the twinkle I see in Ed Galle's eye, and in the eyes of so many others like him whom I have met throughout the Americas. I find great hope in the examples of man's humanity to man. There are people, of all ages and backgrounds, who are giving. In behalf of others, they give their time and skills in education, building, nursing, and applied technology.

Some of these people are giving after-working hours, like the Pillsbury team. Others give full-time. Some help at home and others abroad. Some attract media attention, and others we never hear about. Whoever these people are, the words that they inevitably use to describe their experiences are similar. They say that they receive more than they give. Or, in Ed Galle's words:

> I get a lot of satisfaction out of trying to see if something works. If I can use some of what I have learned to help others, then that is just great.

7. Quinoa Pioneers in the United States

In 1945, food writer Clementine Paddleford discussed "kinoa" in the New York Herald Tribune. A visiting Bolivian agronomist was trying to interest United States food companies in his grain staple. The food companies did not bite; Paddleford did:

> Kinoa cheese pie—that was the best eating. The cooked cereal was mixed with beaten egg as a binder, then layered with grated cheese and baked in a hot oven. We used it as a luncheon main dish . . . .[45]

Following this endorsement, little was heard of quinoa for years. The United Nations Food and Agriculture Organization determined that quinoa was exceptionally nutritious and encouraged its use in the altiplano. There were even some futile attempts to grow it in the United States.

At long last the timing is right for North Americans to embrace quinoa. But quinoa's introduction has not been without the determined perseverance of numerous visionary pioneers. The story of quinoa in the United States is best told by their experiences:

Noel D. Vietmeyer, World Spokesman for Underutilized Foods: As world hunger becomes an increasing concern, scientists look more to ancient cultivars for solutions. Among the many concerned voices, one person skillfully takes the data and breathes life into it. Noel D. Vietmeyer of the National Academy of Sciences is the undisputed spokesman for ancient cultivars. In the past 15 years, Vietmeyer has written over 200 articles for publications ranging from the *Readers Digest* to *Science* magazine.

Vietmeyer's repeated message is to increase our food base by increasing the kinds of foods we eat. He eloquently observes that dependence upon a few elite cultivars is reckless:

> To help feed, clothe, and house an increasing population, to make marginal lands more productive, to meet challenging resource needs, and to reforest the devastated tropics, we need a revitalized worldwide investigation of little-known plant species. Such an effort would expand our agricultural resource base and ease our dangerous dependence on a relative handful of crops. It would build a more stable food supply for drought-stricken Africa and other parts of the Third World, and it would reclothe many of the barren lands where erosion now threatens disaster.[46]

Vietmeyer identifies quinoa as one of the world's most important underutilized foods. He believes that quinoa could become a mainstay of international agriculture. The increasing fascination with exotic fruits and vegetables may be traced, at least in part, to Vietmeyer for he has identified these foods throughout the world. The lush, sweet fruits of Andean origin now appearing in the United States' specialty food markets include *feijoa*, *chirimoya*, and *pepino*. The Andean vegetables with some domestic availability are the yam-like *boniato*, the curious tomato-like *tamarillo*, and a wide array of multi-colored and multi-flavored potatoes. *Tarwi*, the Andean lupine, is available in pasta products. For the most part, these exotic Andean foods are imported.

Introducing an ancient cultivar is a lengthy and laborious process. Making the food available is one step, and garnering consumer attention and acceptance is the second. Recall that soybeans were scarcely used outside of the Orient sixty years ago. Today they are the United States' third-largest crop, and tofu claims shelf space in American supermarkets. Still, many people in the United States are yet to taste tofu. Odds are that it will be some time before a meal of quinoa, tarwi, and tamarillo is as ordinary as a bean and tomato taco. Thanks to the efforts of Noel Vietmeyer and others like him, we are edging in that direction.

Gabriel Howearth, Master Gardener: "I named my daughter, Quinoa, and that says it all," quips Gabriel Howearth. Recognized as a master gardener, Howearth is a vital 36-year-old with an academic background in horticulture. In order to learn traditional gardening Howearth lived, in the mid-seventies, in Central and South America. He worked fields with Indian farmers and collected many seeds, including quinoa. "Seeds," according to Howearth, "are more valuable than gold."

In 1978 Howearth returned to the United States and planted eight quinoa selections in southern Oregon, one of which matured and set seed. This one variety was the first known planting that produced viable seed. Unreported to academic circles, this chenopod was quietly harvested, planted again the next year, and now has a ten-year growing history in the northwest. Howearth is interested in quinoa because:

> Since two-thirds of the world land mass is semi-arid or arid, and since drought and saline soil situations are increasing, we need crops that will thrive in poor soils with minimal rainfall. Of such crops, quinoa has the greatest potential.

Howearth designed the World Peace Garden which lies in the center of the quinoa fields in Crestone, Colorado. Visitors inevitably compare this garden to the magical Findhorn gardens in Scotland, for it radiates vivid color, vitality, and peace.

In the mandala-shaped garden, Howearth has plants arranged according to their area of origin. The garden includes culinary herbs, medicinal, and food plants. Howearth incorporates biodynamic and other techniques in this raised-bed, organic, and sustainable garden. Owing to his deep appreciation for plants, I've found it inspiring to work a row with Howearth.

Dr. Duane Johnson, Colorado State University New-Crops Agronomist: His Levis sporting wide red suspenders, his clothing covered with dust, and quinoa chaff poking from behind his ears, Dr. Duane Johnson climbed down from his combine one afternoon long enough to tell me his part in the quinoa story.

In 1982, Johnson had read that quinoa could not be grown outside the Andes. "Then David Cusack of Sierra Blanca called and said that he had just harvested quinoa in the San Luis Valley (southern Colorado's high mountain valley desert). Cusack wondered if I was interested. You bet I was."

The American farm crisis is rapidly displacing the small and middle-sized farmer. As a university agronomist, Johnson helps regional farmers become, and/or remain, stable. This is no small task. Specialty crops which afford farmers a higher dollar return per acre than do other crops are one answer. Locally grown quinoa is the dream come true of any new-crops agronomist. Johnson relates:

> In 1983, we put in more test plots in the San Luis Valley. We started at absolute zero, we had no idea of what to expect. If I plant wheat I can draw from 2,000 years of wheat growing experience. What little information was available from South America was not always relevant to the different conditions here. We had to learn how deep to plant, how thick to broadcast, how much to water, and much more. Quinoa challenges your imagination.

Johnson reports that just by working on cultural practices he has doubled his yields each year. When a one-half to one percent increase per year is satisfactory for a crop like wheat, then 100 percent annual increases for quinoa are dramatic. He is working to create a quinoa inbred or hybrid. Although hybrids are not self-sustainable, most current farming techniques rely on hybrids because of their increased yields and uniform characteristics.

Stephen Gorad and Don McKinley, Quinoa Corporation: The two men most responsible for creating a quinoa market in the United States are Stephen Gorad and Don McKinley. They first heard of quinoa in 1977 and they would have cooked some on the spot; however, there was none to be found north of the equator.

The next year found Gorad in La Paz, Bolivia, where he promptly purchased quinoa and tried it. "I put it in an open pot and as I watched it cook, I fell in love with it," Gorad said. He sent 50 pounds of quinoa back to McKinley, who equally enjoyed its flavor. The two considered marketing it in the United States, but problems of availability stopped them. Then one morning in 1982, while sitting at his kitchen table, it occurred to McKinley to grow quinoa in Colorado. He enlisted David Cusak's help. As McKinley described it:

> We located David Marsh who was willing to plant a five acre test field at his Center, Colorado, farm. In terms of elevation, lack of moisture, and low temperatures, this San Luis Valley farm approximated growing conditions in the altiplano. Now we just needed the seed.

Gorad, still in Bolivia, looked for seed quinoa. The sketchy supply in local markets had its saponin washed off and therefore would not germinate. Weeks and weeks went by with no luck. Then, Gorad said:

> I had given up on getting seed in time to plant for a 1982 test crop. Then, the day before my flight back to the States a Chilean named Kai Peronard knocked on my

> door with 15 pounds of beautiful pink, yellow, and red seed. In exchange I gave him the shirt off my back. It was a beautiful moment.

The quinoa was planted that spring and harvested in October. They hand-harvested it, hand-threshed it, hand-washed it, and then cooked up a potfull. Gorad recalls with a big smile. "And it was good."

According to agronomists, it would take a minimum of ten years to develop a commercial crop of domestic quinoa. But Cusack was determined to grow it in less time and he pushed ahead with research and development in Colorado. The first commercial quinoa crop of 100,000 pounds was harvested in 1987—only five years after the first planting. Productivity doubled in 1988.

Leaving the domestication of quinoa to others, Gorad and McKinley focused on developing the United States market with imported quinoa. By 1984, imported quinoa was in natural food stores, and four years later it started appearing in supermarkets.

David Cusack and John McCamant, Sierra Blanca Associates: A professor at the University of Colorado, David Cusack joined the efforts of Gorad and McKinley early on, and was a key player until his untimely death at the age of 40, a few years later.

Cusack, the son of a Southern Colorado potato farmer, had married a Chilean woman and spent many years living in South America. His boundless energy was focused on ". . . my dream of an international project bringing together the Rockies and the Andes." He saw that the domestic popularization of quinoa would upgrade the status and availability of this nutritious grain in the altiplano.[47]

After organizing quinoa planting in Colorado, Cusack attended the Fourth International Congress for Andean Crops in Pasto, Columbia. He then traveled to Bolivia to arrange for quinoa germplasm collection and purchase more quinoa. He took a day off to visit the ruins of Tiahuanaco. On June 3, 1984 Cusack sat on the Akapana pyramid and penned a letter to a friend. While there, an unknown assassin shot him in the back with a copper-clad 22-caliber bullet. This letter was retrieved with his personal effects.

> Noon, Tiahuanaco. Just for a moment I write a few lines here at this legendary birthplace of civilization. Am struck by the altitude and vision of grandeur. . . . The land, the clear sky, floating clouds, the wind through dry grass, the cracked red earth and the monolith of a distant past. . . . I feel very peaceful here. Time stops. I almost did not make it here. I have passed several times on route from Puno to La Paz. But luck said, "yes" this time. Some day perhaps we can come here together. If so destined. Autumn soon winter. The wind spirit whispers to me, au revoir.[48]

As reported in the *Denver Post Magazine*, May 4, 1976, David was preparing to expose the U.S. Central Intelligence Agency's role in the overthrow of Chilean President Allende. According to official record, his murder is unsolved.

Dr. John McCamant, a political scientist at Denver University, was David Cusack's dissertation advisor. McCamant picked up the torch that David dropped on his desk, assumed the presidency of David's Sierra Blanca Associates, and vigorously worked to introduce quinoa cultivation to the United States. McCamant has named the prime Colorado quinoa cultivar "David."

Forest Shomer—Quinoa Pioneer in the Northwest: Forest Shomer, one of America's foremost heirloom-seed advocates, is the director of the Abundant Life Seed Foundation in Port Townsend, Washington. Shomer has listed northwestern-grown quinoa seed in his catalog since 1980. His customers, primarily home gardeners, have successfully grown quinoa as far south as the San Francisco Bay area and north into British Columbia. The weather conditions of this region are comparable to coastal Chile, from where Shomer obtained much of his seed. Although historically and presently the bulk of quinoa is grown at high elevations, there are sea level varieties.

Shomer, who terms quinoa as one of the "premier" plants of the Southern Hemisphere, is concerned about those who wish to hybridize and patent it. Said Shomer:

> The plant genes of the world belong to everybody. The way to keep quinoa viable and healthy is to develop many seeds for many different ecosystems and to have viable processing capabilities at the local level.

Emigdio Ballon, Bolivia Agronomist: The former head of quinoa research for the Bolivian Government, Emigdio Ballon, is now working on its cultivation in the United States. Last June, I visited Ballon, who is currently working with the heirloom-seed organization, Talavaya, located in Espanola, New Mexico. Adobe homes and barns intersperse the lush farmland along the cottonwood-lined Rio Grande. The weight of ripening apricots, like little golden suns, bent the boughs low over country lanes as we drove to his garden.

Soft-spoken Ballon taught me ancient planting techniques for desert conditions which, coincidentally, are those used by Hopi Indians today. Though the Inca ruler used a golden planting stick, Ballon's planting stick was simply the closest one at hand.

He broke the soil with the stick, cleared off the first several inches of dry sand and dug down about four inches until he reached damp soil. Then he went another four inches into damp soil, dropped in a pinch of quinoa seeds, and covered it with sand. The seeds lay under a foot of barren-looking soil. "The sand," he said, "acts as a mulch. It keeps the moisture in and controls the weeds."

To demonstrate the effectiveness of deep planting, Ballon pulled up two Hopi bean plants from different parts of his garden. Only their tops were comparable. The conventionally planted and irrigated bean had a one-inch tap root. The deep-planted, dry-farmed bean had a ten-inch tap root. It is common knowledge among farmers that a dry-farmed plant has superior mineral content, flavor, and vitality. Seeing the astounding difference in tap-root length explains why.

In Ballon's home, his wife served blue corn atole, quinoa bread, and coffee while I marveled at Ballon's quinoa seed collection. He has thousands of quinoa samples of all colors and varying sizes. I expected to see the black, brown and buff-colored ones, but not peach-colored seeds or white ones with red eyes.

Ballon also showed me reams of meticulous records with the minutiae of germination, first leafing, blossom time, seed setting, weight, and so on for hundreds upon hundreds of quinoa varieties. This university-trained agronomist confided, "Someday I hope to return to my country and help my people with ancient farming ways."

* * *

Thanks to the efforts of these, and other pioneers, *la chisiya mama* (the mother grain) is available for our enjoyment.

PART II

QUINOA in Your KITCHEN

An Invitation to Cooks: Since quinoa is new to our market, we have just begun to tap its culinary possibilities. If, in preparing any of the following recipes, you encounter difficulty or have suggestions for improving them, I would appreciate hearing from you. Also, I invite you to send your quinoa recipes for testing and possible inclusion (with full credit given) in future editions of this book. Send to Rebecca Wood, in care of:

Japan Publications (U.S.A.), Inc.
45 Hawthorn Place,
Briarcliff Manor, N.Y. 10510

8. All About Cooking Quinoa

Here are the basics about quinoa's performance in the pot and how you can make adjustments to meet your expectations. These directions enable you to substitute quinoa for rice or pasta in almost any recipe. Quinoa proudly stands alone, but it can also be topped with a saffron lobster sauce or stir-fried with vegetables. This ancient grain deliciously stuffs peppers, pears, or partridges. It is an exquisite component of salads and desserts. Quinoa, to say the least, is versatile. And it is quick to prepare.

Saponin: Quinoa seeds are covered with saponin, a bitter-tasting glucoside. Before reaching market, the saponin is either washed off or mechanically removed. However, as quinoa is a new crop to our domestic market, it is not as consistently processed as are other major food commodities, and may thus contain traces of saponin.

A minute amount of saponin seldom causes a problem. A few people—more often children—readily detect and strongly dislike its slightly bitter tang. Large quantities of saponin may irritate the mucous membranes of the intestinal tract and cause diarrhea or other gastrointestinal complaints.

There are two ways to detect saponin. The first is to taste a few grains. A bitter aftertaste indicates the presence of saponin. Or, place quinoa in a bowl and cover it with water. If saponin is present, the water becomes "sudsy." To remove the saponin, simply wash the quinoa until the water runs clean.

Toasting: It is not necessary to toast quinoa prior to cooking. However, toasting brings out a rich, peanut-like taste and gives the grain a lighter "pilaf" texture.

To toast quinoa, place it in a wok or a thin steel pan over a medium-high heat. Cast-iron pots are not recommended; they retain and transfer more heat than steel and excessively dry out the grain. Stir continuously and toast until the grains turn a shade darker and emit a fragrant aroma. Toasting a cup of quinoa takes several minutes and is easily accomplished while the cooking water comes to a boil. For the freshest flavor, wash quinoa and toast just prior to use.

Sautéing: For a richer and heartier dish, instead of toasting, sauté quinoa before cooking it. Allow a minimum of 1/2 teaspoon butter or oil per cup of quinoa. If flavor—rather than calories—is the primary consideration, use up to 1 tablespoon butter per cup of quinoa. Melt butter in a wok or thin steel pan over a medium heat. Add quinoa and sauté until it turns a shade more golden and emits a delicate aroma.

Pressure Cooking: To save time and energy, pressure cook quinoa. For each cup of quinoa, add $1\frac{3}{4}$ cup of water and any seasonings. Bring to full pressure and cook for one minute. Remove from heat and allow pressure to come down by itself. Remove lid and fluff with a fork.

Amount of Water: Most pot-cooked quinoa uses a 1 to 2 ratio of grain to water. (Domestically grown quinoa, however, requires less water; use a $1\frac{1}{2}$ ratio.) This ratio yields grains which are separate and intact. For a creamy breakfast cereal, soup, or pudding increase the water ratio (as much as 1 to 4). This creates a soft, almost "cream-like" texture in which the individual grains swell and burst. For each 1/2 cup additional water over the 1 to 2 ratio, add 10 minutes to the cooking time.

High Altitude Cooking: When cooking quinoa well above sea level, adjust the recipe as follows. At altitudes above 4,000 feet increase the cooking time to 20 minutes. At elevations above 8,000 feet, cook for a total of 25 minutes and increase the water content by 1 tablespoon for every cup of water.

Add Quinoa to Hot or Cold Water: When quinoa is added to boiling water, the cooked grain is separate and fluffy. When added to cold water, a more soft and dense dish is produced. Depending upon the texture you prefer, add quinoa to cold or boiling water.

How to Tell When Quinoa Is Cooked: Quinoa is cooked when the grains are translucent and the crescent-shaped germ separates and becomes white. The periphery of an undercooked strand of spaghetti, relative to its center, is translucent. The same test applies to quinoa. By eye alone, you can see when a grain is completely translucent and, therefore, cooked. Most varieties require 15 minutes cooking at sea level.

For Fluffy Quinoa: When the quinoa has cooked, remove the pot from the stove and allow the quinoa to rest, still covered, for 5 to 10 minutes. This step steams the quinoa, enhances its flavor, and allows it to puff up to its lightest texture. Fluff with a fork and serve as is or combine it with other foods.

Washing Homegrown Quinoa: Unlike other grains, quinoa is easily grown, threshed, and harvested at home without specialized equipment. If you have the good fortune to bring a homegrown variety to table, it requires extra washing attention. There are two methods:

1. *The energy-efficient overnight soaking method is easy.* Place quinoa in a jar, add three times as much water, and allow it to sit for 4 to 10 hours. The quinoa doubles in volume. Pour off excess water. Rinse well and cook. With this method the quinoa absorbs so much soaking water that it has more of a porridge (rather than a pilaf) texture.
2. *Place homegrown quinoa in a washing bag.* Make your washing bag from muslin or use the foot of a nylon stocking. Wash only as much as you will immediately cook. (Wet seeds quickly sprout.) Scrub the bagged quinoa by rubbing it between your hands in a pot of warm water. As the water becomes soapy and cloudy, discard and start with fresh water. Repeat until the water is clear.

Quinoa Solo and in Combination with Other Grains: Below is the basic quinoa recipe as well as recipes for cooking quinoa with other grains. The combination-grain recipes may be used as they are, or they may be substituted in many of the recipes which follow. Preparing quinoa with another grain is economical and results in greater flavor and texture variation.

Quinoa—The Basic Recipe

Unadorned quinoa stands alone beautifully with any meal, and it may be elaborated upon in endless ways. Substitute quinoa for rice or pasta; or use quinoa in soups, salads, breads, and desserts. It enhances other foods with its flavor, texture, and superior nutritional properties.

Yield: 3 cups
Time: 25 minutes

1 cup quinoa
2 cups water
pinch of salt

1. Place the quinoa in a bowl, add warm water for washing, and briefly "scrub" the quinoa between your hands. Using a fine-mesh strainer, pour out washing water, and repeat until the water is clear. Generally, 1 or 2 washings are adequate to remove traces of the bitter saponin.
2. **Optional:** To toast the quinoa, place it in a wok or thin steel pan over a medium heat. Toast for several minutes or until the color is a shade deeper, stirring continuously.
3. Place the water and salt in a 2-quart saucepan and bring to a rapid boil.
4. Add the quinoa to the boiling water, cover, reduce to a simmer, and cook for 15 minutes or until the water is absorbed. Remove from heat. Allow to rest, covered, for 5 to 10 minutes. Fluff with a fork.

Variations:

- Sauté quinoa in unsalted butter or sesame oil (from 1 teaspoon to 1 tablespoon.)
- Add a minced garlic clove, shallot, or 1 small onion.
- Substitute 1 teaspoon natural soy sauce for the salt.
- Add 2 tablespoons of toasted seeds or nuts, such as sesame seeds, sunflower seeds, chopped pecans, walnuts, or hazelnuts.
- Season with 1 tablespoon fresh, or 1/2 teaspoon dried, herbs such as: basil, bay, borage, chervil, cumin, dill, fennel, lovage, marjoram, oregano, parsley, rosemary, saffron, sage, tarragon, or thyme.

See Glossary for descriptions of unfamiliar ingredients.
See Appendix for information on quinoa flour, chilies and natural sugar.

Wild Rice and Quinoa

Who would have imagined that any one ingredient could possibly improve the flavor and appearance of wild rice—and increase its nutritional profile? Quinoa does all of the above, and does it with élan.

Prep Tip: To cook the grains to perfection, set a timer and add the quinoa at precisely the right moment.

Yield: 2 to 4 servings
Time: 1 hour

2½ cups water
1 tsp. natural soy sauce or tamari
½ cup wild rice
½ cup quinoa

1. Bring the water and soy sauce to a boil. Add the wild rice, cover, and simmer for 35 minutes.
2. Add the quinoa, cover, and simmer for 15 minutes or until the water is absorbed. Remove from heat and allow to steam, covered, for 5 minutes. Fluff with a fork.

Variations:
- Use wild rice and quinoa as a stuffing for fish or fowl.
- Place hot wild rice and quinoa into an oiled mold and allow to cool. Remove from mold, garnish, and serve with a rich sauce.
- Turn into a pilaf by adding wild mushrooms, shallots, and fresh, savory herbs.

Corny Quinoa

On sweltering days, corn and quinoa are revitalizing. This combination is so refreshing that, according to my seven-year-old, "It sort of tastes like strawberries." The secrets to obtaining this flavor are double-cutting the corn and using corn stock.

Prep Tip: Double-cut corn kernels readily impart their flavor to the entire dish, while whole kernels tend to retain their flavor.

Yield: 4 servings
Time: 90 minutes

Stock:
3 to 5 corncobs
inner corn husks from 3 to 5 corncobs

1. Place the corncobs, husks, and kombu in a pot, cover with water, and bring to a boil. Cover and simmer for 1 hour or more. Strain out stock. Bring 3 cups stock to a boil in a 1 1/2-quart pot. (Reserve remaining stock for another use.)
2. Meanwhile, double-cut the corn in two easy steps: Grasp an ear of corn in one hand and hold it

1 3-inch strip kombu seaweed
water to cover

Grain:
1 medium ear of corn
$1\frac{1}{2}$ cups quinoa, toasted
1 Tbsp. unsalted butter
$\frac{1}{4}$ tsp. salt

upright on a cutting board. Slice off approximately 50 percent of each corn kernel from the entire cob. Slice again to remove the remaining kernel parts and germ from the cob.

3. Place the quinoa, corn kernels, butter, and salt in the boiling stock, cover, reduce heat, and simmer for 15 minutes or until the liquid is absorbed. Remove from heat and allow to rest for 5 to 10 minutes. Fluff with a fork. Serve.

Variations:

- Add 2 tablespoons chopped poblano chili for a Latin American touch and flavor.
- Top each hot serving of corny quinoa with a tablespoon of grated Monterey Jack cheese. Allow the cheese to melt before serving.
- Convert leftovers into corn chowder.

Millet-Quinoa

Millet is a favorite food of more than the birds (though birds do happen to be the major millet consumers in the United States). It is a staple grain for many African peoples, as well as for many health-conscious Americans. Millet frequently appears as an alternative to rice or as the tasty, nut-like crunch in a whole grain bread. The flavors and textures of millet and quinoa marry well.

Yield: **2 to 4 servings**
Time: **40 minutes**

$2\frac{1}{2}$ cups water
pinch of salt
$\frac{1}{2}$ cup millet
$\frac{1}{2}$ cup quinoa
2 Tbsp. sunflower seeds, toasted

1. Bring the water and salt to a boil. Add the millet, cover, and simmer for 15 minutes.

2. Add the quinoa and sunflower seeds, cover, and continue to simmer for another 15 minutes or until the water is absorbed. Remove from heat and allow to rest, covered, for 5 to 10 minutes. Fluff with a fork. Serve.

Variations:

- Prepare a double recipe and press half into an oiled casserole. Allow to cool thoroughly, slice, and pan-fry like polenta. Season with natural soy sauce and serve as a lunch side dish, or top with a hot maple syrup glaze (page 160) and serve for breakfast.
- To make curry, add 1 small onion, diced, and 1 teaspoon curry powder.

Buckwheat and Quinoa

Buckwheat, the most warming and hearty of grains, combines with the lighter quinoa to form a duo that is especially suitable for winter eating. Enjoy this combination with milk and honey for breakfast, or pan-fried for a lunch-time croquette. Or, dress it to the hilt with an elegant sauce.

Prep Tip: If you are using chestnut-colored, roasted buckwheat (*kasha*), you may omit toasting (step 1). For maximum flavor, I begin with white-green unroasted buckwheat and toast it before cooking.

Yield: 4 to 6 servings
Time: 20 to 25 minutes

1 cup unroasted buckwheat
1 cup quinoa, washed
4 cups water
$\frac{1}{8}$ to $\frac{1}{4}$ tsp. salt

1. Place the buckwheat in a wok or a thin skillet and toast over high heat, stirring continuously, until it turns an amber color and emits a deep aroma. Remove the buckwheat and next toast the quinoa until it turns a shade darker in color.
2. Place the water and salt in a 2-quart saucepan and bring to a boil. Add the quinoa and then the buckwheat. Do this slowly to prevent the water from bubbling over. Cover and simmer for 15 minutes or until the water is absorbed. Allow to rest for 5 to 10 minutes. Fluff with a fork. Serve.

Variations:
- Add 1 diced shallot and 1 teaspoon unsalted butter to the cooking grain.
- Add 1/2 cup green peas during the last 3 minutes of cooking.

Cooked quinoa

9. Breakfast Foods

Quinoa-Stuffed Red Bartlett Pears

Do not peel the pears—the skins seal in the juices and flavor. But do serve the pears while they are still warm, since their skins will shrivel as they cool. The minted quinoa stuffing raises the fruit to aristocratic heights, though not many dishes are easier to assemble. In fact, children can have fun taking charge.

Yield: **4 servings**
Prep time: **15 minutes, using cooked quinoa**
Total time: **1 hour, 15 minutes**

4 red Bartlett pears
12 mint leaves
½ cup cooked quinoa
½ cup walnuts, finely chopped
several grains of salt
⅛ tsp. ground cloves
¼ cup honey
2 Tbsp. currants

1. Preheat oven to 350°F.
2. With an apple corer, remove cores from pears by slicing in from the bottom.
3. Mince 8 of the mint leaves. Combine with the quinoa, walnuts, salt, cloves, honey, and currants.
4. Stuff the pears. Set them upright in a glass or ceramic baking dish and bake, uncovered, for 1 hour. Garnish with the remaining mint leaves and serve.

Variations:
- Substitute 2 drops of mint extract for the fresh mint.
- Substitute 1 teaspoon of red miso for the salt.
- Substitute apples, firm yellow Bartlett pears, or Anjou pears for the red Bartletts. Omit the cloves and add 1/4 teaspoon cinnamon.
- Steam the pears instead of baking them.
- Substitute raisins for the currants and serve the pears with raisin sauce.
- Substitute raspberry jam for the currants. Thin additional jam to make a sauce.
- Splash with pear liqueur before serving.

Blood Orange-Avocado-Quinoa Salad

Serve this salad for brunch, as a dramatic dinner salad, or even for dessert. The color and texture combinations of the ingredients will captivate the most jaded gourmet.

Yield: **4 servings**
Time: **10 minutes, using cooked quinoa**

2 blood oranges

1. Slice oranges crosswise, then slice a thin strip of peel from the bottoms to enable each half to remain upright. Reserve the strips of peel. Using a serrated, curved grapefuit knife, remove the sections of fruit. Scrape out remaining membranes and

1 avocado
1 cup cooked, cooled quinoa
2 Tbsp. fresh lime juice

reserve the juice.
2. Peel, remove pit, and dice the avocado. Toss with the orange sections, reserved juice, quinoa, and lime juice. Fill orange cups with mixture and garnish with the sliced peel.

Variations:
- Substitute grapefruit for the orange.
- Add toasted seeds or nuts or unsweetened coconut flakes.
- Substitute cantaloupe or honeydew melon for the oranges.
- Garnish with a dollop of yogurt or sour cream.

Oat Bran Quinoa Pancakes

Quinoa and healthful oat bran team up to rejuvenate an old breakfast friend, the pancake. Deeply golden, they are blessed with a cake-like lightness and a spunky orange flavor. Pancakes made of whole-grain flour and vegetable oil (rather than white flour and butter) tend to be gummy and heavy, but not these high-rising beauties. Wheat-free, they will be especially appreciated by those who are allergic to wheat.

Prep Tip: This batter is thick and yields a higher-than-average pancake which cooks and browns in record time. Flip pancakes before the air bubbles pop and the surface dries.

Yield: 12 4-inch pancakes
Time: 20 minutes

1 cup quinoa flour
1 cup oat bran
¼ tsp. salt
3 Tbsp. natural sugar
2 eggs
3 Tbsp. sesame oil
1 cup milk
⅓ cup orange juice
1 tsp. orange zest

1. Combine the flour, bran, salt, and sugar in a medium-sized mixing bowl.
2. In a separate bowl mix eggs, oil, milk, juice, and zest. Mix with dry ingredients. Stir just to blend (overmixing will yield a tough crumb).
3. Pour about 1/3 cup batter per pancake onto a hot, seasoned skillet or griddle. Cook the first side just until air bubbles form and the bottom is golden. Turn and briefly cook the other side until golden. Serve hot with butter or softened rice syrup.

Variations:
- Add up to 1 cup of cooked and cooled quinoa to the wet ingredients.
- Substitute barley or buckwheat flour for the quinoa flour.
- Wrap pancakes around creamed chicken or seafood.

Upside-Down Asian Pear Pancake

A sweet topping of tender Asian pear slices and crunchy almonds crowns this puffy-light dessert pancake. It is impressive-looking—and deceptively easy to prepare. I serve upside-down Asian pear pancake for a special breakfast, a brunch, afternoon tea, or as a dessert.

Prep Tip: If you are serving this pancake as a dessert, measure the ingredients in advance. Then you can quickly cook it after the meal.

Yield: 1 pancake, 4 servings
Time: 25 minutes

Pancake:
- **½ cup quinoa flour**
- **½ tsp. baking powder**
- **pinch of salt**
- **2 egg yolks**
- **¼ cup milk**
- **2 egg whites**
- **½ tsp. cream of tartar**

Topping:
- **2 Tbsp. unsalted butter**
- **2 Tbsp. maple syrup**
- **1 tsp. ginger juice**
- **3 Tbsp. blanched and slivered almonds**
- **1 large ripe Asian pear, peeled and cut into ¼-inch slices**

1. Preheat oven to 400°F.
2. Combine the flour, baking powder, and salt.
3. Lightly beat the egg yolks in a large bowl. Stir the milk into the yolks. Add the flour mixture to the liquid ingredients and mix well. Set aside.
4. To make the topping, melt the butter in a 7-inch skillet. Add the maple syrup and ginger juice and mix. Arrange the almond slivers and Asian pear slices in the skillet and cook, without stirring, over low heat for about 7 minutes or until the mixture starts to brown.
5. Meanwhile, beat the egg whites and cream of tartar at high speed until peaks are formed. Gently fold into the batter. Pour batter over cooked peaches and smooth the surface. Bake in a pre-heated oven until golden brown and a toothpick inserted near the center comes out clean, about 12 minutes. Loosen the edges of the pancake with a spatula. Invert the pancake on a serving plate. Cut into wedges.

Variations:
- Use other fruits such as blueberries, cherries, sliced bananas, peaches, pears, or plums.
- Substitute oat bran for half of the quinoa flour.

Ableskivers (Danish Pancakes with Quinoa)

This is my mother's recipe, via her Danish grandmother, embellished with quinoa. Ableskivers (AH bla SKEE-vers) are a nifty finger food that are fun to eat. Each golden pancake is the size and shape of a golf ball, but has a hollow inside like a popover. Open the steaming sphere, add a dab of butter, a dollop of jam, and savor.

Ableskiver pans have seven round wells for the batter; they sell for about seven dollars in cookware shops. With a little practice and a seasoned pan, it is easy to form perfect ball shapes.

Yields: 28 ableskivers (4 servings)
Time: 30 minutes

1 cup quinoa flour
1 cup unbleached white flour
1 Tbsp. natural sugar
2 tsp. baking powder
1 tsp. cardamom, powdered
¼ tsp. salt
2 eggs
1½ cups milk
1 Tbsp. unsalted butter, melted
½ tsp. lemon zest

1. Sift together the two flours, sugar, baking powder, cardamom, and salt.
2. Beat the eggs. Add the milk, melted butter, and lemon zest. Mix. Stir into dry ingredients and beat just enough to make a smooth batter.
3. Heat an ableskiver pan over medium heat. Thoroughly oil wells. Fill each well 5/8 full of batter and allow to cook for several minutes or just until the surface contacting the pan has browned. With a bamboo skewer (or thin knitting needle or nut pick), pierce and lift the cooked side up to a right angle. The batter pours out to form a second surface. When the new surface browns, turn again. A total of four turns produces a round and hollow ball. Serve hot.

Variations:
- Add a small *skiver* of apple before making the first turn. This addition explains the Danish name ("apple slice") and provides a tasty, hidden treasure. A blueberry, or other fruit, may be substituted for the apple slice.
- Use the same quantities of buttermilk and soda in place of the milk and baking powder.

Buttermilk-Sunflower Waffles

What I like about these surprisingly light waffles is the nutritional boost that whole quinoa bestows. The crunch of sunflower seeds gives these waffles pizzaz.

Yield: about 6 waffles
Prep time: 10 minutes
Total time: 30 minutes

1 egg
1¼ cups buttermilk
2 Tbsp. sesame oil
1½ cups whole wheat pastry flour

1. Preheat waffle iron.
2. In a blender, blend the egg, buttermilk, and oil. Add the flour, baking soda, and salt. Blend just until smooth.
3. Stir cooked quinoa into batter, using a spatula to break up any lumps.
4. Sprinkle each heated and oiled waffle-iron square with 1 tablespoon of the sunflower seeds.

1 tsp. baking soda
¼ tsp. salt
1 cup cooked, cooled quinoa
1 cup raw, unsalted sunflower seeds

Pour the batter onto the seeds, then quickly sprinkle the surface of the batter with another tablespoon of sunflower seeds. Close the waffle iron. Bake until steam stops escaping and the waffle comes away from the iron. Repeat with remaining batter and seeds. Serve with butter and maple syrup glaze (see page 160) or honey.

Variations:
- Substitute 3/4 cup of quinoa or barley flour for 3/4 cup of the whole wheat pastry flour.
- Substitute other seeds such as: poppy, sesame, chia, or flax for the sunflower seeds.

Chocolate Quinoa Waffles

These exceedingly rich and tender waffles make a memorable dessert for a brunch or any other meal.

Prep Tip: For a superior waffle, prepare batter from 2 to 8 hours in advance. Cover and refrigerate until ready to use.

Yield: about 4 waffles
Time: 20 minutes

Waffles:
1 oz. unsweetened chocolate
¼ cup unsalted butter
¾ cup quinoa flour
1 tsp. baking powder
¼ tsp. salt
¼ tsp. cinnamon
¼ tsp. nutmeg
½ cup natural sugar
1 egg
¼ cup milk
½ tsp. vanilla

Topping:
1 cup yogurt
pomegranate seeds

1. In a small, heavy saucepan melt the chocolate and butter over low heat. Stir as necessary. Allow to cool.
2. Preheat waffle iron.
3. In a medium-sized mixing bowl combine the flour, baking powder, salt, cinnamon, nutmeg, and sugar. Set aside.
4. Beat the egg in a small bowl. Stir in the milk, vanilla, and the cooled chocolate and butter mixture. Combine with dry ingredients, stirring just enough to mix.
5. Bake until steam stops escaping and the waffle comes away from the iron. Serve hot, topped with yogurt and pomegranate seeds.

Variations:
- For dessert serve waffles—hot or cold—with a scoop of ice cream rather than yogurt.
- Sandwich whipped cream between two waffles.

Quinoa Crêpes with Black Sesame Seeds

Their paper-thinness contributes an element of whimsy to these elegant crêpes. Enjoy them for breakfast, brunch, or supper. Steamed vegetables, often ignored by children, are eagerly eaten when wrapped in a crêpe. Fish, fowl, or fruit concoctions also make good crêpe fillings.

Prep Tip: Crêpes turn out best when the batter has been prepared several hours, or even a day ahead of time. If cooked crêpes are not for immediate consumption, allow them to cool, then stack them between layers of waxed paper or parchment paper and cover with an airtight wrap.

Yield: 8 10-inch crêpes
Time: 30 minutes

1 cup quinoa flour
¼ cup unbleached white flour
¼ tsp. salt
2 cups milk
1 egg, beaten
1 Tbsp. unsalted butter, melted
1 Tbsp. black sesame seeds

1. Combine the quinoa flour, white flour and salt in a medium-sized mixing bowl and set aside.
2. Beat together the milk, egg and butter. Stir the wet ingredients into the dry ones, being careful not to overmix.
3. Heat a crêpe pan and brush with butter. Grasp the pan in one hand and pour about 1/3 cup batter onto pan. While pouring, rotate the pan so that the batter spreads and covers the pan's surface in a paper-thin layer. Immediately sprinkle with a few black sesame seeds. Cook for 3 minutes or until lightly browned. Turn and cook for an additional minute.

Variations:

- For a dairy-free crêpe, substitute soy milk for the milk, and sesame oil for the butter.

Fluffy Eggs with Quinoa

In the Western world, soft yellow eggs are a traditional way to start the day. Quinoa adds fiber and textural interest. If you prefer, the proportions can be reversed to yield scrambled quinoa with egg: the quinoa contributes fluffiness and the egg binds.

Yield: 2 to 4 servings
Time: 10 minutes, using cooked quinoa

2 tsp. unsalted butter
½ cup mushrooms, thinly sliced

1. Heat an 8-inch skillet and add the butter. Over a medium heat sauté the mushrooms for 2 to 3 minutes.
2. Add the scallions and quinoa. Cook, stirring occasionally, for 3 minutes or until quinoa is evenly heated.

3 scallions, sliced into ¼-inch rounds
1 cup cooked quinoa
3 eggs
¼ tsp. salt
2 Tbsp. natural Worcestershire sauce

3. In a small bowl mix the eggs, salt and Worcestershire sauce. Add the egg mixture to the skillet. Stir briskly with a fork and cook over medium heat for 2 minutes or just until the eggs set. Do not overcook.

Variations:

- To increase the volume without increasing cholesterol, add 3 egg whites.
- Mince and add 1/2 Anaheim chili and substitute 1/4 cup grated Monterey Jack cheese for the salt.

Chicken Liver-Quinoa Breakfast Patties

Serve these sausage-like patties with waffles, grits, hash browns, or eggs. Maple syrup brings out their hearty flavor. Or try a topping of black cherry conserves or marmalade thinned to a sauce consistency.

Yield: 1 dozen patties
Time: 20 minutes, using cooked quinoa

1 cup cooked, cooled quinoa
1 egg white
½ lb. chicken livers
1 shallot, quartered
¼ tsp. salt
safflower oil for pan frying

1. In a medium mixing bowl, thoroughly combine the quinoa and egg white.
2. Place livers, shallot, and salt in a food processor and process until smooth. Add to the quinoa-egg white mixture.
3. Heat a skillet and add oil. Drop the thick batter by the tablespoon onto the skillet, gently press with a spatula to form a 3/4-inch-thick patty. Cook over medium heat until browned, about 3 minutes, then turn and cook the other side until browned.

Variation:

- Replace chicken livers with the following: 1 cup tofu (with water squeezed out), 2 tablespoons flour, 2 tablespoons nutritional yeast, 2 teaspoons tamari, 1/2 teaspoon ground celery seed, and 1 chopped scallion. Form into 6 patties.

Creamy Crock Pot Porridge

Let time and your kitchen equipment do the cooking for you. Put up this porridge the night before and awaken to the comforting aroma of hot cereal. Milk, maple syrup, and butter are traditional New England toppings.

Yield: 4 to 6 servings
Time: 6 to 9 hours

½ cup barley
½ cup quinoa
pinch of salt
4 cups water

Place all ingredients in a crock pot, set on high heat, cover, and simmer overnight.

Variations:

- Replace barley with one of the following: brown rice, whole oats, wheat or rye berries, millet, triticale, or posole.

Leafy Grain Trio—Amaranth, Buckwheat, and Quinoa

Winter weather calls for substantial dishes, such as this blend of the three leafy grains. Botanically, amaranth, buckwheat, and quinoa are not true cereal grains, but each boasts a superior nutritional profile and is non-allergenic. These broad-leafed plants carry wide appeal: amaranth contributes a nutty and wild note; buckwheat, a hearty tone; and quinoa a distinctive light texture. Serve this cereal with milk and honey—or eat it plain.

Prep Tip: Make a generous portion for breakfast and incorporate the leftovers into a stir-fry, croquettes, casserole, salad, or yeasted bread.

Yield: 4 to 5 servings
Time: 25 minutes

½ cup kasha (toasted buckwheat)
½ cup quinoa
2 Tbsp. amaranth
3 cups water
pinch of salt

Place all the ingredients in a 1½-quart pot and bring to a boil. Cover and simmer for 25 minutes or until the water is absorbed. Remove from heat. Stir to evenly distribute the grains.

Variation:

- For a sweeter cereal, add raisins and a dash of cinnamon.

Fruited 5-Grain Cereal

Eating a multi-grain porridge for breakfast starts the day off right, especially when the weather is brisk. I consider combinations of five grains to be the maximum for any single preparation. (Those with delicate digestive systems may wish to keep to three grains, and to replace the apple juice with water.) Using six or more grains results in a confusing mix.

Yield: 3 to 4 servings
Time: 30 minutes

Place all ingredients in a 1 1/2-quart pot. Cover and bring to a boil. Reduce heat and simmer for 30 minutes or until the cereal is creamy. Toward the

3 cups apple juice
¼ cup oat groats
¼ cup quinoa
¼ cup kasha
¼ cup bulgur
¼ cup millet
¼ cup raisins (or currants)
¼ cup almonds, chopped
¼ tsp. cinnamon
⅛ tsp. salt

end of cooking, stir occasionally to prevent scorching.

Variation:

- Substitute corn grits, couscous, teff, quick-cooking brown rice, or cracked rye.

Quinoa-Enriched White Bread (page 147)

10. Comeda De Dedo
(Finger Food)

Stuffed Banana Peppers

Serve stuffed peppers as an elegant tapas, hors d'oeuvres, or side dish. If this sweet pepper, also known as Hungarian yellow wax pepper, is unavailable, the Cubanelle is comparable. For a spicy dish substitute Anaheim chilies.

Prep Tip: The feta and quinoa filling may be prepared 1 to 2 days in advance. Allow the filled chilies to stand at room temperature for one hour prior to serving.

Yield: 6 peppers
Time: 25 minutes, using cooked quinoa

6 banana peppers, blistered, steamed, and peeled
½ cup feta cheese, crumbled
⅔ cup cooked, cooled quinoa
¼ cup extra virgin olive oil
2 Tbsp. minced fresh oregano (or 1 tsp. dried)

Garnish:
fresh oregano sprigs

1. Make a slash along one side of the peppers and remove seeds.
2. In a small bowl combine the cheese, quinoa, oil, and oregano. Stuff each pepper. Roll the pepper to completely enclose the filling. Arrange peppers seam-side down. Garnish with oregano sprigs.

Variations:

- For a low-cholesterol cheese and low-fat version, use tofu instead of the feta. Allow tofu mixture to ripen one day before stuffing peppers.
- For another low-cholesterol, low-fat version, stuff with quinoa hummus (see page 89) rather than with the feta-quinoa mixture.

Radîcchio Cups with Quinoa-Tofu Filling

Brash magenta-colored radîcchio leaves make stunning and sturdy leaf-cups for tapas or appetizers. Their bittersweet flavor and crisp texture plays off against the rich and succulent filling of quinoa and tofu.

Prep Tip: Prepare the filling a day in advance and refrigerate. Hold filling at room temperature 1 hour prior to serving to allow flavor to mellow. If the tofu is not subtly sweet, parboil it first. Bring 2 cups of lightly salted water to a boil. Slice the tofu into 1-inch slices and add it to the boiling water. Boil for 30 seconds, remove, and drain.

Yield: 5 servings
Time: 5 minutes, using cooked quinoa

½ cup tofu
1 cup cooked quinoa
¼ cup minced fennel stalk and

1. Crumble the tofu into a mixing bowl. Mix in the remaining ingredients, except for the radîcchio.
2. Spoon the filling into each radîcchio leaf and arrange on a platter or on individual plates.

See Glossary for descriptions of unfamiliar ingredients. See Appendix for information on quinoa flour, chilies and natural sugar.

frond
1 shallot, minced
2 Tbsp. minced sweet yellow pepper
2 Tbsp. finely chopped chives
1 Tbsp. ume vinegar (or lemon juice and salt to taste)
2 Tbsp. extra virgin olive oil
$\frac{1}{8}$ tsp. freshly ground black pepper
6 radicchio leaves

Variations:

- Substitute Gorgonzola, cottage or Roquefort cheese for the tofu.
- Substitute hard-boiled eggs for the tofu and mayonnaise for the olive oil. Add 1 tablespoon prepared mustard.
- Substitute drained sweet relish or minced sweet gherkin pickles for the yellow pepper.

Caviar, Summer Squash, and Quinoa

A diversity of flavors, colors, and textures comes together in these miniature bowls. Crisp squash skins hold the smooth white filling, which is flavored with herbs and topped with salty caviar and lemon.

Prep Tip: For the best texture and maximum flavor, use garden-fresh yellow summer squash.

Yield: 10 to 12 cups
Time: 15 minutes, using cooked quinoa

1 avocado
1 cup cooked, cooled quinoa
2 Tbsp. minced fresh dill weed (or 1 tsp. dried)
1 Tbsp. fresh, minced rosemary (or $\frac{1}{2}$ tsp. dried)
$\frac{1}{4}$ tsp. salt
4 to 5 medium, perfect yellow squash
1 tsp. red caviar
1 tsp. black caviar
1 lemon, sliced into thin wedges

1. Peel and pit the avocado. With a fork, mash it with the quinoa, dill weed, rosemary, and salt. Mix until smooth.
2. Slice 1/1/2-inch crosswise slices from the center of the squashes. Reserve ends for another use. Using a melon baller, hollow each chunk from one side to form a thin-walled bowl.
3. Fill the bowls with avocado-quinoa mixture. Top half of the cups with red caviar, the remaining with black caviar. Serve with lemon wedges.

Variations:

- Omit the caviar. Increase salt to 3/4 teaspoon and top with fresh, slivered cucumber peel.
- Substitute other fresh herbs for the dill and rosemary. Tarragon, savory, thyme, coriander, and chives work well.
- Substitute zucchini, cucumbers, or small tomatoes for the summer squash.

Parmesan Quinoa Fritters

These fritters are inspired by those served at the popular tapas restaurant in New York, the Ballroom. They make excellent hors d'oeuvres or may be served as a side dish with dinner. The zesty condiment which accompanies them is a digestive aid for oil-rich foods.

Prep Tip: The mixture may be prepared several hours in advance.

Yield: **18 to 20 small fritters**
Time: **20 minutes, using cooked quinoa**

2 cups cooked quinoa
¼ cup grated Parmesan cheese
¼ cup minced shallots
3 Tbsp. minced parsley
¼ tsp. salt
¼ tsp. white pepper
¾ cup peanut oil

Condiments:
¼ cup grated daikon
1 Tbsp. natural soy sauce or ume vinegar

1. In a bowl, combine the quinoa, Parmesan cheese, shallots, parsley, salt, and white pepper.
2. Heat the oil in either a wok or deep skillet until it is fragrant but not smoking. Shape the mixture into small patties or log shapes. Gently drop into the hot oil one at a time. Do not overcrowd the wok or skillet. Fry until golden on all sides. Remove from the oil and drain on paper towels. Serve hot.
3. Place daikon in a small container and stir in natural soy sauce or ume. Serve alongside fritters.

Variations:

- Add scraped corn kernels. Use fresh cilantro instead of the parsley, and grated cheddar cheese instead of the Parmesan. Serve with tomato salsa.
- Roll in toasted sesame seeds and bake at 350°F. for 25 to 30 minutes.
- Instead of the Parmesan cheese, use well-drained tofu, crumbled and seasoned with salt or natural soy sauce.
- Replace quinoa with a mixture of either quinoa and millet, or quinoa and buckwheat.
- Pan-fry rather than deep-fry.

Norwegian Cheese Squares

Gjetöst is a goat cheese made from caramelized whey. It releases a variety of subtle and strong flavors that play over the palate one at a time. These Gjetöst squares can be prepared in advance and are easily transported to a party or a picnic.

Yield: 24 to 30 1-inch squares
Prep Time: 15 minutes, using cooked quinoa
Total Time: 35 minutes

1 cup grated Gjetöst cheese
$1\frac{1}{2}$ cups cooked, cooled quinoa
2 eggs, separated
3 to 6 dashes natural hot pepper sauce (or Tabasco)
$\frac{1}{4}$ tsp. paprika

1. Preheat oven to 350°F.
2. Combine the cheese, quinoa, egg yolks, and pepper sauce.
3. Whip the egg whites until stiff but not dry. Fold into the cheese-quinoa mixture. Pour into an oiled glass loaf dish. Sprinkle with paprika. Bake for 20 minutes. Cool. Slice into 1-inch squares.

Variations:
- Substitute 3 tablespoons dried chives for the paprika.
- Substitute juice of grated onion for the pepper sauce.
- Bake in a pie shell; cut into thin slices.

Cajun Snacks

I am not going to claim these as authentic southern Louisiana appetizers, but they certainly could be. Not for the timid of tongue, Cajun snacks enliven drinks of any persuasion.

Prep Tip: Freshly cooked quinoa can easily be molded into shapes. For stars, moons, leaves and other simple, fanciful forms, press the quinoa mixture into 1-ounce rubber or tin candy molds.

Yield: 48 1-inch balls
Prep time: 15 minutes
Total time: 45 minutes

$1\frac{1}{2}$ cups water
$\frac{1}{8}$ tsp. salt
$\frac{3}{4}$ cup quinoa
1 cup pecans
1 tsp. red pepper flakes
1 tsp. liquid smoke
1 tsp. natural soy sauce or tamari
$\frac{1}{4}$ tsp. granulated garlic
$\frac{1}{4}$ cup coarse-grained mustard

1. In a saucepan, bring the water and salt to a boil. Add the quinoa, reduce heat, cover, and cook over low heat for 20 minutes.
2. Meanwhile, process the pecans in a processor or nut grinder until they are very fine.
3. When the quinoa is cooked, and while it is still hot, stir in the pecans, red pepper flakes, liquid smoke, soy sauce, garlic, and mustard. Continue mixing until the quinoa is cool enough to handle.
4. Preheat oven to 350°F.
5. Shape into 1-inch balls. Place on oiled baking sheets and bake for 15 minutes. Serve warm or at room temperature.

Variations:
- Omit baking, for a softer, quicker snack.
- Substitute pine nuts, almonds, walnuts, or cashews for the pecans.
- Deep-fry the quinoa balls

Star Canapés with Tofu-Caper Topping

Tempeh, originally from Indonesia, is a fermented food made from soybeans and, often, one or more grains. Like its unfermented counterpart, tofu, it is enhanced by a variety of seasonings. Quinoa tempeh is available in many natural foods stores as a "gourmet" item. It is a delicately sweet and lightly aromatic product.

These crisp stars with their savory topping make appetizing canapés. Unadorned, the stars are a high-protein item for a youngster's lunchbox. They are most crisp when freshly made.

Prep Tip: The flavor of the tofu topping is improved if prepared a day in advance and refrigerated in an airtight container. For the crispiest tempeh, allow cut pieces to sun-dry for 15 minutes prior to cooking.

Yield: 12 2-inch stars
Time: 20 minutes

Stars:
- **1 10-ounce package quinoa tempeh**
- **1 tsp. ground coriander**
- **½ tsp granulated garlic**
- **1 Tbsp. natural soy sauce or tamari**
- **½ cup coconut milk or water**
- **½ cup rice flour or arrow-root flour**
- **¼ cup peanut oil for shallow frying**

Topping:
- **½ cup Tofu-Caper Topping (recipe follows)**

Garnishes:
- **lemon zest**
- **fresh chervil sprigs**
- **poppy seeds**

1. Cut tempeh through the center to form two thin sheets the same shape as the original rectangle. Using a star-shaped cookie cutter (approximately 2 inches in diameter), cut stars from each tempeh sheet. Reserve leftover pieces for another preparation. Mix coriander, garlic, soy sauce, and coconut milk in a shallow bowl. Allow tempeh stars to rest in the milk mixture for several seconds, then dust them with flour.
2. Heat the oil in a wok or a deep skillet over medium heat until it is hot and fragrant but not smoking. Add 4 to 5 stars. Fry the stars for 1 1/2 to 2 minutes on each side or until they are crisp and golden brown. Drain well on paper towels.
3. Top each star with a teaspoon of Tofu-Caper Topping and one or two suggested garnishes. Arrange on a platter and serve.

Variations:
- Cut the tempeh into fingers.
- Combine yogurt, mustard, and honey for a dipping sauce. Omit the tofu topping.

Tofu-Caper Topping

Prep Tip: If tofu is not absolutely fresh, parboil it as per instructions in Radîcchio Cups (see page 84).

Yield: 1/2 cup
Time: 5 minutes

4 oz. firm tofu
1 clove garlic, pressed or minced
2 Tbsp. extra virgin olive oil
1 Tbsp. white wine or mirin
pinch of salt
pinch of freshly ground black pepper
1 Tbsp. capers
2 Tbsp. minced red bell pepper

Place tofu in a clean muslin cloth and squeeze out water. Blend squeezed tofu and all ingredients, except capers and bell pepper, until smooth. Taste and adjust seasonings. Transfer to a bowl and stir in capers and bell pepper. Refrigerate in an airtight container for a day.

Quinoa Hummus

Traditional Middle Eastern hummus is substantial and zesty. The quinoa version is a lighter dish but has an even richer texture and flavor. Serve hummus on chapati or other breads as a sandwich filling. To make canapés, stuff raw vegetables with it or dab it onto a cracker.

Prep Tip: For the flavors to blend, prepare quinoa hummus an hour in advance and allow to stand at room temperature.

Yield: 3 cups
Time: 5 minutes, using cooked garbanzos and quinoa

1½ cups cooked garbanzos
1½ cups cooked quinoa
2 Tbsp. tahini
¼ tsp. salt
1 Tbsp. fresh lemon juice
½ tsp. cumin seeds
1 clove garlic, minced or pressed

Garnishes:
fresh cilantro sprigs
paprika

1. Set aside 1/4 cup of the garbanzos to use as a garnish.
2. Place the remaining garbanzos, quinoa, tahini, salt, lemon juice, cumin, and garlic in a food processor and purée. Place in a serving bowl. Garnish with whole garbanzos, cilantro, and paprika.

Variations:

- Substitute olive oil for the tahini and garnish with chopped olives.
- Using garbanzo cooking liquid, thin hummus to a dip consistency and serve with chips or vegetable sticks.

Quinoa Temaki

Hand-rolled sushi fits American eating styles because it is so easy to make, delicious, and attractive. Unlike sushi, which requires the use of a sushi mat and the expertise of a skilled chef, anybody can roll a *temaki* or a hand-roll. This new quinoa variation is the inspiration of chef Yuji Matsumura of Denver, Colorado's Sushi Den—a charming restaurant.

Prep Tip: Purchase the best nori available—inexpensive nori is too fragile. Prepare the hand-rolls to order in the sushi-bar tradition. For the most potently flavored *wasabi*, mix it 10 to 15 minutes before serving.

Yield: 6 rolls
Time: 10 minutes

Dip:
2 Tbsp. wasabi powder
½ tsp. lukewarm water

Hand-roll:
3 sheets folded nori
¾ cup cooked quinoa
½ cup fresh, cooked crab
6 ⅛-inch-wide slices avocado
6 ¼-inch pieces shaved celery

1. Mix the wasabi and water, cover, and set aside.
2. Open the sheet of nori. Re-fold it in half, at right angles to the original fold, to create two 7-1/2 by 4-inch pieces. Again open flat, turn it over, and repeat over the newly made fold. Tear or cut along this crease. Repeat with the other two nori sheets. Lay all six pieces of nori on the counter.
3. On the left half of each nori piece arrange (see illustration) the quinoa, crab, avocado, and celery. Lay the filled quinoa sheet on the palm of your left hand. Tuck and wrap the bottom left corner of the sheet around the food ingredients. Now roll the remaining nori to make a cone shape. Dip finger tip in water and moisten inside the nori seam to seal the edge. Lay the cone on a serving platter with the edge down. Place the wasabi in a tiny condiment dish and serve with the temaki.

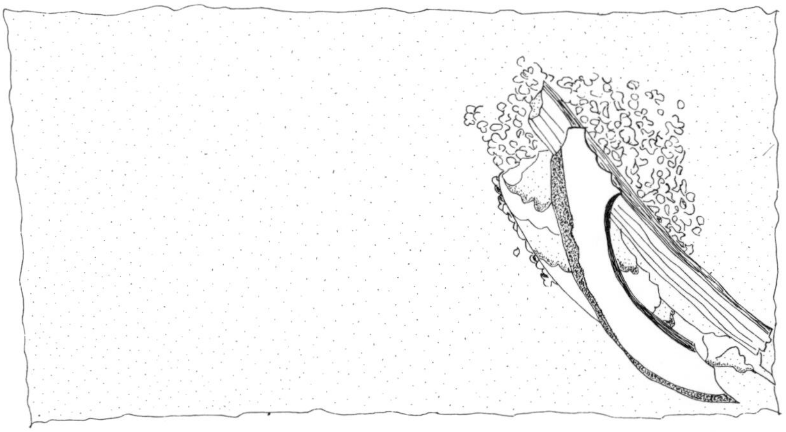

#1

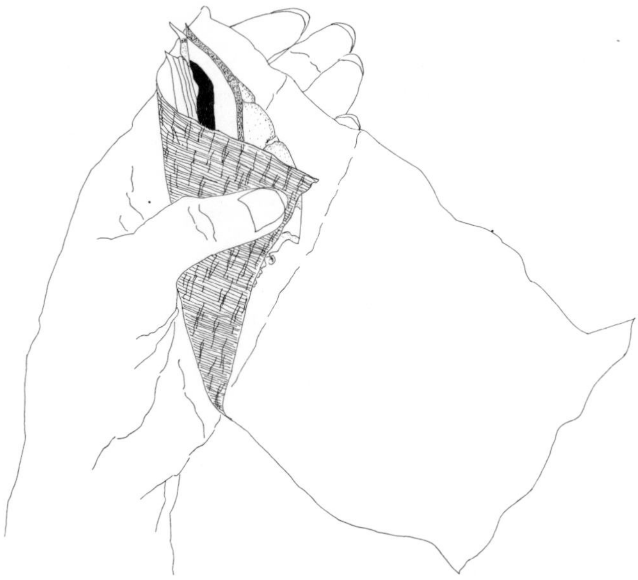

#2
Quinoa Temaki Illustration 1, 2 & 3.

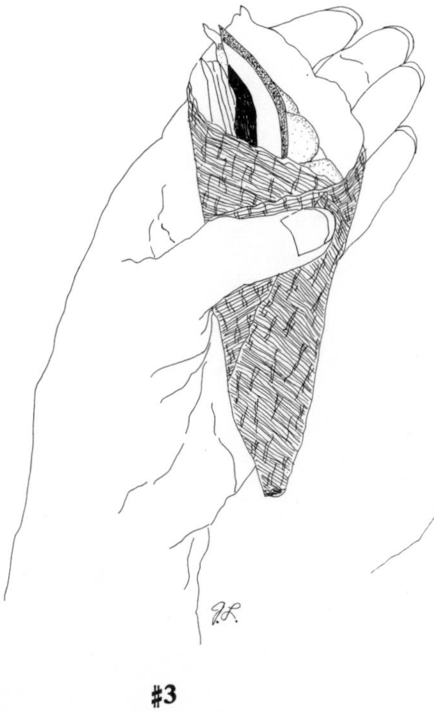

#3

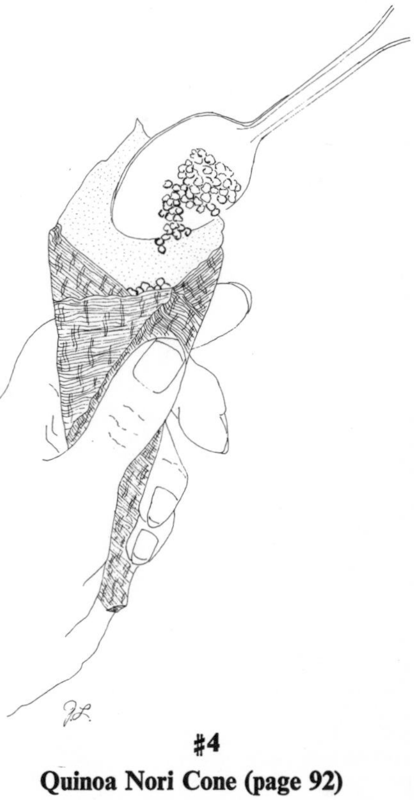

#4
Quinoa Nori Cone (page 92)

Quinoa Nori Cones

Nori cones are a standard quick snack or lunch in our home and a favorite of the neighborhood children. Unlike the prepared hand-rolls (see recipe above), these are filled in hand and eaten out of hand. Don't be put off by the long list of ingredients below. They are merely suggestions. Odds are that, once you get the hang of it, you will quickly and easily make quinoa cones with nori, quinoa, and an assortment of fillings gleaned from your refrigerator and/or the pantry shelf.

Yield: **2 cones**
Time: **2 minutes, using cooked quinoa and prepared ingredients**

1 sheet nori seaweed
¼ cup cooked quinoa

Filling (select one):
cooked fresh shrimp
fried salmon skin
diced chicken breast
tempeh, marinated and fried

Topping (select one):
carrot, finely grated
pickled ginger
prepared salad dressing
cucumber, thinly sliced
sauerkraut

1. Tear the nori sheet into two 7 1/2 by 4-inch pieces (see step 2 of preceding recipe). Roll one of them into a cone shape.
2. Hold cone in hand. Layer approximately 2 tablespoons quinoa, 1 tablespoon of a filling, and 1 teaspoon of a topping into cone. Eat out of hand.

Quinoa Dolmadakia (Stuffed Grape Leaves)

Dolmadakia disappear like lightning at parties. They call for fresh grape leaves, though bottled vine leaves or collard greens will substitute. Quinoa enhances this traditional Greek dish, which is typically served with a bowl of chilled yogurt.

Yield: **18 dolmadakia**
Time: **1 hour 15 minutes**

2 Tbsp. zante currants
2 Tbsp. dry white wine
2 Tbsp. extra virgin olive oil
¼ cup quinoa

1. In a small bowl combine the currants and wine. Set aside for 5 minutes.
2. Heat a skillet, add 1 tablespoon of olive oil and sauté the quinoa for several minutes or until it becomes lightly browned. Add and lightly sauté the chives, cilantro, fennel, and pine nuts. Add currants along with their soaking liquid, and salt. Cover and

¼ cup chopped chives
2 tsp. finely chopped fresh cilantro
⅓ cup minced fennel
2 Tbsp. pine nuts
⅛ tsp. salt
18 grape leaves
juice of lemon
1 cup vegetable stock

Garnish:
lemon wedges

simmer until the liquid is absorbed, about 5 minutes. Remove from skillet and spread out on a plate to allow to cool.

3. While quinoa mixture is cooking, prepare the grape leaves. If using canned leaves, scald with hot water and drain. If using fresh leaves, wash. Cut off stems of either fresh or canned leaves. Pat dry, and place on paper towels with shiny surface down. Place 1 teaspoon of cooled quinoa mixture in the center of each leaf. Fold stem end of leaf over to cover filling; fold up sides of leaf and roll over carefully until a cylinder about 2-inches long is formed. Repeat until all the leaves are filled.

4. Place the remaining tablespoon of olive oil in a pot. Layer dolmadakia in pot. Add lemon juice to stock and pour over dolmadakia. Fit a smaller lid or plate on top of the stuffed grape leaves to provide a little weight. Cover pot and simmer over very low heat for 45 minutes or until the liquid is absorbed. Remove, drain, and cool before serving. To serve, arrange stuffed leaves on a platter garnished with lemon wedges.

Variations:

- Arrange rolls in a casserole and bake in a 350°F. oven for 45 minutes.
- Substitute minced parsley and mint leaves for the cilantro and fennel.

Huminta with Calamata Olives

Huminta is a popular Bolivian quinoa "tamale." Like a tamale, it is wrapped inside corn (or banana) leaves and steamed. Humintas vary from region to region but typically are *dulce* (sweet) or *sal* (salty). Anise flavors the sweet humintas and the salty—or savory—ones may contain a pork morsel, peanuts or, as in the following recipe, an olive. Humintas travel well.

Pre Tip: Annatto seeds, available in specialty food shops, are used for flavor and color. They may be omitted for a less authentic, but no less delicious, rendition. If corn husks are dry, rehydrate in water for 1 to 2 hours prior to use. Humintas stay fresh in the refrigerator for several days. They also freeze well when wrapped tightly. Steam refrigerated or frozen humintas to warm them before serving.

Yield: 8 tamales
Prep time: 15 minutes, using cooked quinoa
Total time: 1 hour

10 corn husks
1 Tbsp. unsalted butter
¼ tsp. annato seeds
¼ tsp. cumin seeds
1 tsp. red chili powder
pinch of freshly ground black pepper
1 clove garlic, minced or pressed
1 medium onion, diced
3 cups cooked quinoa
8 calamata olives

1. Remove any silk from the corn husks. (Rehydrate husks if they are dried.)
2. Melt the butter in a skillet over a low flame and sauté the annato seeds until the oil turns a vivid scarlet-orange. Remove seeds with a slotted spoon and discard. Add the cumin, chili powder, and black pepper. Sauté the garlic and onion until limp, about 5 minutes. Add the quinoa and lightly sauté, about 3 minutes.
3. Divide the quinoa mixture among the 8 widest corn husks. (Cut the remaining husks into 1/2-inch strips to use as ties.) Spread the quinoa mixture to 1 inch from the wide-ended bottom, and halfway up towards the pointed top. Leave a 3/4-inch border along the sides.

Place an olive in the center of the filling. Fold the sides of the husk together to cover the filling. Fold the huminta in half and tie it at the top with a husk strip. With scissors, clip off surplus husk and ends of tie. Repeat until all humintas are assembled.

4. Place the humintas in a steamer and steam for 35 minutes. Serve hot, in the husk.

Variations:

- Vary the huminta filling by adding any of the following: seitan, tofu, chicken, beef, cooked beans or tempeh.
- For huminta *dulce*, season the quinoa with a sweetener, raisins, and anise.

Seaburgers

Nori seaweed's mild ocean flavor mingles easily with the quinoa, and pita makes a perfect pocket. These super-nourishing seafood sandwiches are dramatically colored and taste great.

Pre Tip: Since pita bread is all crust, it usually tastes stale. Here's how to freshen it: Bring to a boil a small amount of water in a large pot with a steaming rack. Remove from heat and arrange unsliced pita on rack. Replace lid and let sit a few minutes or until pita is pliable and thoroughly warmed.

Yield: 2 sandwiches
Time: 35 minutes

1. In a saucepan, bring the water and salt to boil. Add the quinoa, cover, reduce heat, and cook over

1½ cups water
⅛ tsp. salt
¾ cup quinoa
½ cup green nori flakes
¼ cup kelp powder
1 Tbsp. sesame oil
¼ cup mayonnaise
1 Tbsp. fresh grated horseradish
1 tsp. ume vinegar
2 rounds of whole wheat pita bread
4 leaves endive
1 medium tomato, sliced into thin cresents

low heat for 20 minutes. While quinoa is still hot, stir in the nori flakes and kelp powder. As soon as the mixture is cool enough to handle comfortably, shape it into 4 patties.

2. Heat a skillet, add the oil, and pan-fry the patties over medium heat for 4 to 5 minutes on each side. Remove and drain on paper towels or on a rack.

3. Combine the mayonnaise, horseradish, and ume vinegar.

4. Slice the pita breads in half crosswise. Open the pockets and spread an equal amount of the mayonnaise mixture in each. Add quinoa patty, endive, and sliced tomato.

Variations:

- Substitute avocado mashed with salt and lemon juice for the hoseradish mayonnaise.
- Serve the burgers on burger buns, sliced bread, or simply on a plate topped with the flavored mayonnaise and accompanied by the endive and tomatoes, or by another green salad.
- Shape the warm quinoa mixture into 1 1/2-inch balls and serve as party snacks on frilled toothpicks with a chili sauce as a dip.
- Add 2 tablespoons toasted sunflower seeds to the quinoa mixture.

Cajun Snacks (page 87)

11. Soups, Chowders, and Stews

Porcini Dumplings in Chilled Zucchini Soup

This thick, bright-green purée with savory quinoa islands afloat in it captures the spa-food spirit. It is low-fat and low-salt, but high-carbohydrate, high-fiber, and certainly high-flavor. The quinoa supplies strong protein and the seaweed stock delivers both a natural monosodium glutamate and plenty of minerals. For serious dieters, the butter can be reduced to a smidgen. Superb when chilled, this soup is equally good served hot.

Prep Tip: Make the soup 3 to 24 hours before serving and chill quickly, uncovered, for best flavor and color.

Yield: 4 to 6 servings
Prep time: 1 hour
Total time: 5 hours

Soup:
- **3 cups water**
- **1 4-inch piece kombu seaweed**
- **6 medium zucchinis**
- **½ Tbsp. minced fresh oregano (or ½ tsp. dried)**
- **1 tsp. salt**

Dumplings:
- **1 tsp. unsalted butter**
- **6 medium mushrooms (common supermarket variety), diced fine**
- **6 fresh (or dried and rehydrated) porcini mushrooms, diced fine**
- **½ tsp. salt**
- **¾ cup vegetable stock**
- **½ cup quinoa**

1. Place the water and kombu in a soup pot. Slice the zucchinis lengthwise and then into 1/2-inch slices. Add to the water with the oregano and salt. Bring to a boil. As soon as the water boils, remove the kombu and discard or reserve for another use. Cover and simmer over low heat for 10 minutes.
2. Meanwhile, prepare the dumplings. Heat a skillet over medium heat and add the butter. Add the common mushrooms and sauté for 5 minutes, then add the porcini mushrooms and salt, and cook until all the liquid has cooked away. Add the stock and bring it to a boil. Add the quinoa, cover, and cook over low heat for 20 minutes. Remove from heat and stir until the mixture is cool enough to handle. Shape into 16 to 18 1 1/2-inch dumplings. Allow to cool for 30 minutes. Cover and refrigerate.
3. Purée zucchini soup in a blender until smooth. Chill.
4. Portion the soup into soup bowls. Carefully slide chilled quinoa dumplings into each serving.

Variations:
- Substitute young beets, carrots, summer squash, or cucumbers for the zucchini.
- Cook the zucchini in the 3 cups of water, and purée when cooled with 1 ripe avocado or 1 cup light cream.
- Substitute fresh dill, basil, lemon grass, cilantro, summer savory, or sorrel for the oregano.

See Glossary for descriptions of unfamiliar ingredients. See Appendix for information on quinoa flour, chilies and natural sugar.

Pasta, Shrimp, and Snow Peas in Kombu Dashi

The clear stock indispensable to traditional Japanese cuisine is the soy sauce and seaweed-based *kombu dashi*. Its aromatic, pungent flavor greatly enhances pasta, vegetables, and shrimp. Serve this Japanese-style soup in large bowls, for it is a complete and nourishing meal in itself.

Prep Tips: This meal-in-a-bowl can be pulled together quickly if some of these foods are already on hand: cooked pasta, kombu seaweed stock, and lightly steamed vegetables such as broccoli, watercress, lotus root, or *shiitake* mushrooms.

Yield: 4 portions
Time: 1 hour

Kombu Dashi:
- **1 4-inch piece kombu seaweed**
- **3 cups water**
- **1 Tbsp. natural soy sauce or tamari**
- **½ tsp. salt**
- **1 tsp. ginger juice**

Pasta:
- **3 qt. water**
- **1 Tbsp. salt**
- **4 oz. flat quinoa pasta (about 2 cups)**
- **2 Tbsp. toasted sesame oil**
- **few drops red pepper oil**

Toppings:
- **20 snow peas**
- **12 medium-sized shrimp, boiled, shelled, and deveined**
- **1 scallion, slice into long, diagonal slivers**

1. Add the kombu to the water and set aside.
2. Bring the pasta cooking water with salt to a boil. Add the pasta, stir, and cook for 15 minutes or until it is tender but not mushy. Drain. Toss well with toasted sesame oil and red pepper oil.
3. Meanwhile, bring the kombu and water to a boil. Just when the water boils, remove kombu (discard or reserve for another use). Reduce heat and add the soy sauce and salt. Add the ginger juice, snow peas, and shrimp to the kombu stock and simmer for 3 to 5 minutes or until the peas are just cooked and the shrimp are heated through. Remove peas and shrimp with a slotted spoon and allow them to drain.
4. Divide the pasta among 4 large soup bowls. Arrange shrimp and snow peas on top of pasta. Ladle hot broth over pasta and garnish with scallion slivers. Serve hot.

Variations:
- Substitute miso to taste for the soy sauce and salt.
- *Mochi* (pounded sweet rice) may be purchased or prepared fresh; bake or deep-fry and substitute it for the shrimp.
- Substitute ginger powder to taste for the freshly grated ginger root. Substitute a few grains of cayenne pepper (add them to the stock) for the red pepper oil.
- Use *soba* or *udon* instead of the quinoa pasta.
- Use tofu, *aburage* or seitan for the shrimp.

Quinoa Clouds in Hot and Sour Broth

Delicate puffs of quinoa cook on the surface of this piquant soup. An ideal start to a cold weather meal, it warms the body from the inside out, and whets the appetite the Oriental way.

Yield: **4 servings**
Time: **15 minutes, using prepared chicken stock**

4 cups chicken stock
1½ Tbsp. natural soy sauce or tamari
2 Tbsp. brown rice vinegar
several grains cayenne
1 egg, separated
¼ cup cooked, cooled quinoa

Garnish:
4 sprigs fresh cilantro

1. In a 1 1/2-quart soup pot combine the chicken stock, soy sauce, vinegar, and cayenne. Bring to a boil, reduce heat, and simmer over low heat for 5 minutes. Taste the broth and correct the seasoning.
2. Combine the egg yolk and quinoa. Beat the egg white until stiff but not dry. Fold into the quinoa mixture.
3. Gently spoon the egg/quinoa mixture onto the surface of the simmering soup. Cook, uncovered, over low heat for 5 minutes or just until the mixture sets.
4. Ladle the broth into 4 bowls, dividing the "clouds" evenly among bowls. Garnish each with a cilantro sprig.

Variations:
- Substitute vegetable, fish, or seaweed stock for the chicken stock.
- Cook the quinoa clouds on top of an herbed chicken soup, a chunky vegetable stew, a light miso broth, a smooth vegetable purée, or a tomato bisque.

Sauerkraut Soup with Quinoa and Garbanzos

Whether you put up your own sauerkraut or buy it already made, soup is a novel way to enjoy it. Both quinoa and garbanzos provide a counter-taste to the main ingredient. If a thinner soup is desired, use just the juice from drained kraut. Homemade or naturally fermented bottled kraut is preferred. If you use unsalted kraut, flavor the soup with salt to taste.

Prep Tip: The best vegetable stock for this soup is made from the cooking liquid from the garbanzos plus sweet vegetables such as onions, carrots, parsnips, winter squash, and corncobs.

Yield: 4 servings
Prep Time: 15 minutes, using cooked garbanzos
Total Time: 45 minutes

1 Tbsp. unsalted butter
1 medium onion, very thinly sliced
1 cup undrained sauerkraut
2 cups vegetable stock
¼ cup cooked garbanzos
¼ cup quinoa

Garnish:
herbed garlic bread croutons

1. Heat a heavy soup pot, add the butter, and sauté the onion until it is sweet and limp, about 15 minutes.
2. Add the sauerkraut, stock, garbanzos, and quinoa. Bring to a boil, cover, reduce heat, and simmer for 30 minutes. Garnish with croutons.

Variations:
- Briefly toast caraway, dill, or fennel seeds in butter before adding the onion.
- Substitute sauerkraut juice for the sauerkraut, add diced carrots and corn kernels.
- Substitute white beans for the garbanzos.
- Add cooked chicken or turkey and substitute poultry stock for the vegetable stock.
- Substitute roasted red-skinned peanuts for croutons.

Sopa de Quinoa y Tomate

In South America quinoa is considered an "Indian" food, and is not available in restaurants. This recipe is based on a white rice soup which I was served in a vegetarian restaurant in the Peruvian city of Cusco. I am sure that similar quinoa soups are savored in rural homes throughout the altiplano.

Yield: 4 to 6 servings
Time: 45 minutes

1 Tbsp. extra virgin olive oil
1 Tbsp. fresh chopped borage (½ tsp. dried)
1 clove garlic, minced or pressed
1 medium onion, diced
½ cup green beans, tipped and sliced into 1-inch pieces
2 stalks celery, chopped into ½-inch pieces
2 cups tomatoes, peeled, seeded, and chopped
½ tsp. salt
6 cups vegetable stock
½ cup quinoa

Garnish:
1 avocado, peeled and sliced
6 wedges lime

Heat a 2-quart soup pot. Add the oil and lightly sauté in the following order: borage, garlic, onion, green beans, celery, and tomatoes. Add the salt, stock, and quinoa. Cover the pot, bring to a boil, reduce heat, and simmer for 30 minutes. Adjust seasonings. Ladle the soup into bowls. Garnish each bowl with avocado slices. Serve hot with lime wedges on the side.

Variation:
- Substitute cod (add it the last 5 minutes) for green beans; and use fish stock instead of the vegetable stock.

Creamy Burdock Miso Soup

Earthy-sweet burdock makes a wonderful partner for quinoa. If the long, brown root, also called *gobo*, is not available, you may substitute salsify for a similar effect. Contrary to popular opinion, neither root requires peeling; to do so wastes nutrients and flavor.

Yield: **4 servings**
Time: **35 minutes**

Soup:
- **½ tsp. sesame oil**
- **1 medium burdock root, diced (about ½ cup)**
- **1 3-inch strip wakame seaweed**
- **½ cup water**
- **¾ cup finely sliced celery and celery leaf**
- **1 medium onion, diced**
- **¼ cup quinoa**
- **1 bay leaf**
- **4 cups vegetable stock**
- **¼ cup white miso**

Garnish:
- **scallion slivers**

1. Add the sesame oil to a 1 1/2-quart soup pot and sauté burdock for several minutes.
2. Meanwhile, rehydrate the wakame in the water for 3 minutes or until soft. Cut out center stipe (stem) and reserve for soup stock. Chop remaining fronds into fine pieces. Add wakame and soaking water, celery, onion, quinoa, bay leaf, and vegetable stock to the burdock. Bring to a boil, cover, reduce heat, and simmer for 30 minutes.
3. Remove 1/2 cup stock from the soup and use it to purée the miso. Add puréed miso to soup and gently stir to blend ingredients. Allow to simmer, uncovered, for 30 seconds, then remove from heat. Remove bay leave. Garnish.

Variations:
- Substitute turnip, rutabaga, or daikon for the burdock.
- Add 1/3 cup diced poultry or tofu.

Spiced Cream of Garlic Soup

The stock for this smooth potage is based on toasted sweet spices and cream. Quinoa's soft beads thicken the soup and provide textural interest.

Yield: **4 servings**
Prep Time: **15 minutes**
Total Time: **1 hour**

Stock:
- **1 tsp. unsalted butter**
- **1 tsp. coriander seeds**
- **1 tsp. mustard seeds**
- **1 tsp. whole cloves**
- **4 cups water**

1. Heat the soup pot over medium heat. Add the butter and toast the coriander seeds, mustard seeds and cloves for 1 minute. Add water, salt, onion, cinnamon, and ginger root. Cover and simmer for 30 minutes. Strain and discard spices and onion.
2. Return the stock to the soup pot. Add the garlic, quinoa, and wine. Bring to a boil, cover, reduce heat, and simmer over low heat for 20 minutes.

1 tsp. salt
1 small onion, diced
1 stick cinnamon
1-inch piece fresh ginger root, thinly sliced

Soup:
10 to 12 medium cloves garlic, minced or pressed
½ cup quinoa
¼ cup sauterne wine
1 cup half-and-half cream

Garnish:
¼ tsp. freshly ground nutmeg

3. Add the half-and-half. Heat through. Add a dash of nutmeg to each bowl and serve.

Variations:
- Serve the soup chilled. It thickens as it cools.
- Add scallops, clams, or crabmeat during the last five to ten minutes of cooking.
- Substitute cooked and puréed winter squash or soymilk for half-and-half.

Cream of Turkey Soup

The cream in this recipe is actually quinoa, which softens and blends easily with the other ingredients to make a soothing, melt-in-your-mouth soup. Use fresh sage if available. If not, use fresh parsley, marjoram, oregano, thyme or rosemary. Frozen herbs are second choice with dried herbs a distant third.

Yield: 4 to 6 servings
Time: 1 hour

1 Tbsp. unsalted butter
1 small onion, minced
1 clove garlic, minced or pressed
2 ribs celery, minced
½ tsp. salt
6 medium mushrooms, minced
1 medium carrot, diced
1 Tbsp. minced fresh sage (or ½ tsp. dried)
8 cups turkey stock
1 cup diced turkey
½ cup quinoa
1 tsp. salt, or to taste

1. Heat a heavy-bottmed soup pot and add the butter. Sauté the onion, garlic, celery and the 1/2 teaspoon salt over medium heat until the onion is translucent, about 5 minutes. Add the mushrooms and carrot and continue sautéing for an additional 5 minutes.
2. Add the sage, stock, turkey, quinoa and the remaining 1 teaspoon of salt. Simmer 30 to 40 minutes.

Variations:
- Substitute any other poultry for the turkey.
- Substitute a strong-flavored white fish such as cod for turkey and season with onion, oregano, and cayenne.
- Add additional vegetables such as rutabagas, kale, cabbage, and parsnips.

Quinoa Corn Chowder

Yes, there are delicious, nourishing, and attractive soups that fall together easily and quickly, and this is one of the best of that class. You can improve its flavor by using stock made from boiled corn husks, silks, and/or cobs. If cooked quinoa is used, reduce the cooking time to 10 minutes.

Yield: 4 to 6 servings
Time: 45 minutes

1 Tbsp. unsalted butter
1 large onion, chopped
2 cloves garlic, minced or pressed
3 cups corn kernels
½ cup quinoa
4 cups vegetable stock
1 bay leaf
½ tsp. salt
2 cups milk
½ cup diced red bell pepper
2 Tbsp. fresh dill weed (or 1 tsp. dried)
freshly ground black pepper to taste

Garnish:
sprigs of fresh dill or parsley

1. Heat the butter in a soup pot. Sauté the onion, garlic, corn, and quinoa. Add the stock, bay leaf, and salt; bring to a boil, cover, and simmer for 30 minutes.
2. Add the milk, red bell pepper, dill and black pepper. Simmer an additional 5 minutes. Adjust the seasonings. Garnish and serve.

Variations:
- Purée the soup in a blender; serve chilled.
- Replace the milk with soymilk or with half-and-half cream.
- Add a large red potato, peeled and cubed, when the stock is added.

Traditional Altiplano Quinoa Chowder

The two primary staples of the Bolivian altiplano are *chunos* and quinoa. *Chunos* are naturally freeze-dried potatoes. When fresh, these multicolored spuds are much sweeter than North American varieties. When reconstituted and cooked, they are just as delicious and have a water chestnutlike crunch. This otherwise typical altiplano chowder calls for fresh potatoes rather than *chunos*.

Yield: 4 servings
Prep Time: 10 minutes
Total Time: 40 minutes

1. Heat the butter over a medium heat in a heavy soup pot. Add the pork and brown lightly. Add the onion, garlic, salt, and pepper, and sauté until the vegetables are limp, about 5 minutes. Add quinoa, potatoes, jalapeño, and stock. Bring to a boil,

1 Tbsp. unsalted butter
meat (and bone) from 1 pork chop, trimmed of fat and cubed
½ cup chopped onion
1 clove garlic, minced or pressed
½ tsp. salt
freshly ground black pepper to taste
½ cup quinoa
2 cups diced potatoes
1 jalapeño chili, blistered, steamed, peeled and diced
6 cups stock
½ cup peanuts
½ cup milk
2 egg yolks, beaten

cover, and simmer for 30 minutes.
2. Remove the soup bone. Chop the peanuts in a food processor, then mix with the milk and egg yolks. Stir into the soup. Adjust seasonings. Serve hot.

Variations:
- Substitute poultry or tofu for the pork.
- Substitute peeled, seeded, chopped tomatoes for the milk and omit the eggs.

Kabocha Stew

In terms of the number of ingredients, this is not your usual stew; in terms of texture and rustic goodness, it qualifies. The *kabocha* squash (also known as Hokkaido pumpkin) has a dense texture and is meltingly sweet. It is not peeled, so small flecks of green skin add both flavor and color. Buttercup, butternut, golden nugget, or turban squash may be substituted.

Yield: 4 servings
Prep Time: 10 minutes
Total Time: 40 minutes

Soup:
1 Tbsp. unsalted butter
1 small onion, diced
2 cups kabocha squash, diced small
½ cup quinoa
4 cups vegetable stock
1 Tbsp. natural soy sauce or tamari
1 Tbsp. chopped fresh tarragon (½ tsp. dried)
½ tsp. salt

Garnish:
chopped chives

1. Melt the butter in a heavy soup pot. Sauté the onion, squash, and then quinoa. Add the stock, soy sauce, tarragon, and salt, and bring to a boil. Cover and simmer for 30 minutes.
2. With 5 to 10 strokes of a potato masher or ricer, purée most of the squash to create a stewlike consistency. Adjust seasonings. Garnish and serve.

Variations:
- Substitute marjoram or basil for the tarragon.
- Substitute 2 tablespoons puréed white miso for the salt and soy sauce.
- Purée 2 tablespoons tahini with one cup soup, return to soup and cook for 1 minute.

Lentil-Quinoa-Parsnip Stew

The old fashioned parsnip combines well with the humble lentil and visually exciting quinoa. For a well-balanced meal, serve this unpretentious stew with a hunk of bread, and a simple salad. Make extra—it is even better the next day.

Prep Tip: A plump, unpeeled parsnip increases the fiber and the flavor of this soup. If the parsnip is not absolutely fresh, its skin will be bitter and should be discarded. If the parsnip is past its prime, substitute turnip, rutabaga, burdock, salsify, or carrot.

Yields: 4 to 6 servings
Time: 45 minutes

1 cup lentils
3 cups water
1 strip kombu seaweed
1 Tbsp. sesame oil
1 bay leaf
1 Tbsp. minced savory (½ tsp. dried)
1 leek, sliced into ½-inch pieces
2 cloves garlic, minced or pressed
2 ribs celery, thinly sliced
1 large parsnip, diced
½ cup quinoa
2 cups vegetable stock
2 Tbsp. natural soy sauce or tamari
¼ tsp. salt

Garnish:
rye bread croutons

1. Place the lentils, water, and kombu in a pot and bring to a boil. Remove from heat and allow to sit for 2 to 8 hours.
2. Heat the oil in a heavy soup pot and sauté the bay leaf, savory, leek, garlic, celery, parsnip and quinoa. Remove kombu from the lentils and dice it. Add kombu, lentils, and cooking liquid to the soup pot. Add the stock, bring to a boil, cover, and simmer for 30 minutes. Season with the soy sauce, salt, and pepper, and cook an additional 5 minutes. Adjust seasonings. Garnish.

Variations:

- Substitute red lentils, navy, anasazi, bolita, pinto, or cranberry beans for the lentils.
- Substitute roasted or hot sesame oil for the sesame oil.
- Pressure-cook lentils and kombu for 45 minutes and eliminate the 2 to 8 hour soak.

12. An Assortment of Salads

Quinoa Greens, Arugula, Enoki, and Mung Bean Noodles

Tender young quinoa leaves make a delectable spinachlike salad green. (The commonplace weed, lamb's-quarters, is a close cousin and may be substituted.) Ethereal mung-bean noodles, delicate *enoki* mushrooms and nippy arugula are other components of this refreshing springtime salad that actually doubles as a purifying spring tonic.

Yield: 4 servings
Time: 10 minutes

Salad:
- **4 oz. mung bean noodles (harusame)**
- **3 cups quinoa greens**
- **3 cups arugula greens**
- **¼ lb. enoki mushrooms**
- **1 Tbsp. chopped fresh chervil**

Dressing:
- **1 Tbsp. white miso**
- **2 Tbsp. fresh lemon juice**
- **1 Tbsp. hazelnut (or walnut) oil**

1. Drop noodles into a quart of boiling water and cook for 4 minutes or until tender. Remove and immediately rinse under cold running water. Set aside.
2. Trim root mass from the enoki. Quickly rinse the mushrooms, drain, and blot dry. Set aside.
3. Prepare vinaigrette in a small jar. Purée the miso with the lemon juice. Add the hazelnut oil. Secure jar with a lid and shake vigorously until emulsified.
4. On four plates compose the greens, noodles, enoki, and chervil. Pour 1 tablespoon dressing over each salad.

Variations:
- If quinoa greens are not available, use another tender wild green such as miner's lettuce, chickweed, wild mustard, cress, or chicory.
- Garnish with edible flowers. Flowers that can be eaten include: violets, roses, nasturtiums, daylilies, and cucumber, bean, thyme, oregano, and chive blossoms.
- Substitute other transparent noodles such as *beifun*, *kuzu-kiri* or rice vermicelli for the mung bean noodles.
- Substitute radîcchio, watercress, Belgian endive or Bibb lettuce for either the quinoa greens or the arugula.
- Substitute fresh burnet, coriander, lovage or marjoram for the chevil.

See Glossary for descriptions of unfamiliar ingredients. See Appendix for information on quinoa flour, chilies and natural sugar.

Quinoa Fruit Salad

Creamy quinoa anchors this unusual lunch or breakfast salad that depends for the most part on colorful, tropical fruits for its variety of flavors. Toasting the poppy seeds may seem like a chore, but it improves their flavor noticeably. The poppy seeds echo the look and crunch of the kiwi seeds, creating a leitmotif for this composition.

Prep Tip: If serving as a breakfast salad or dessert, you may wish to omit the lettuce and warm the salad, covered, in a 350°F. oven for 15 minutes.

Yield: 2 servings
Prep Time: 15 minutes
Total Time: 1 hour

1 cup milk
½ cup quinoa
few grains of salt
¼ cup poppy seeds
1 Tbsp. tupelo honey
1 tangerine
12 cherries
1 kiwi fruit
1 banana
4 to 6 lettuce leaves

1. Place the milk, quinoa, and salt in the top part of a double boiler, cover, and cook over boiling water for 30 minutes, or until all the milk is absorbed by the quinoa.
2. Meanwhile, heat a wok over medium heat, add the poppy seeds and stir for about 30 seconds. Remove wok from heat and pour the seeds into a small bowl to cool.
3. With a fork, stir the honey into the cooked quinoa. Fluff the quinoa and allow it to cool. Fluff again and chill.
4. Peel and section the tangerine, removing all white membranes. Remove stems from cherries. Peel and slice the kiwi fruit. Peel and slice the banana into rounds.
5. Arrange the lettuce leaves on two plates. Divide the quinoa between the two lettuce beds. Arrange the tangerine sections, cherries, kiwi, and banana slices on each salad. Sprinkle poppy seeds over fruit.

Variations:

- Almost any fruit will complement the quinoa. Some possibilities include: apple and pear wedges with raisins; pineapple chunks with grapefruit and orange sections; and grapes, watermelon, and cantaloupe.
- Substitute soymilk for the milk.

Noodle Salad with Fresh Soy Mayonnaise

Not many salads meet the specifications of this one: substantial enough to be the focus of a meal, impressive enough for entertaining, and pretty and tasty enough to be devoured by children. If you have a choice, use tart (rather than sweet) star fruit.

Yield: **2 servings**
Time: **45 minutes**

Salad:
- **5 qt. water**
- **1 tsp. salt**
- **4 oz. quinoa flat pasta (about 2 cups)**
- **1 medium-sized red bell pepper**
- **½ cup shelled green peas**
- **1 small star fruit**
- **6 to 8 Bibb lettuce leaves**

Dressing:
- **½ cup soymilk**
- **½ cup safflower oil**
- **2 Tbsp. minced fresh chives (or ½ tsp. dried)**
- **2 Tbsp. minced fresh mint (or ½ tsp. dried)**
- **1 tsp. brown rice vinegar**
- **½ tsp. salt**
- **¼ tsp. mustard powder**

1. Bring the water and salt to a boil. Add the pasta, stir, and cook for 15 minutes, until the pasta is tender but not mushy. Drain and cool.
2. Halve the red pepper. Remove the seeds, stem, and any white pulp. Sliver lengthwise. Peel star-fruit ribs and slice across to form thin stars. Steam the peas until they are tender but still a bright green. Cool all ingredients.
3. Place the soymilk, oil, chives, mint, vinegar, salt, and mustard powder in blender and blend until smooth and thick. If the dressing is too thin, slowly pour in a stream of additional oil (with blender motor still operating) until it thickens. Pour over pasta and gently mix to evenly coat the pasta.
4. Arrange lettuce leaves on two plates and divide the pasta between the two lettuce beds. Arrange the red-pepper slivers, star-fruit slices, and peas in clusters around the pasta. Serve chilled.

Quinoa Marinated with Oil-Cured Olives

The conquering Spaniards introduced olive trees to California as well as to South America. According to food pundit Waverly Root, three trees were planted in Lima, Peru, in 1560, one of which was later stolen and transplanted to Chile. Today the olive, which happily allies with quinoa, is an indispensable ingredient in both North and South American cuisines.

Prep Tip: This salad is even better when prepared a day in advance.

Yield: **4 servings**
Prep Time: **5 minutes, using**

1. Toss together the quinoa, black and green olives, scallions, parsley, and oregano.

cooked quinoa
Total Time: 1 hour

Salad:

- **4 cups cooked, cooled quinoa**
- **½ cup oil-cured black olives, pitted and sliced**
- **½ cup dried oil-cured green olives, pitted and sliced**
- **3 Tbsp. thinly sliced scallion**
- **3 Tbsp. minced fresh parsley**
- **3 Tbsp. minced fresh oregano (or 1½ tsp. dried)**
- **8 escarole leaves**

Dressing:

- **2 Tbsp. fresh lemon juice**
- **3 Tbsp. extra virgin olive oil**
- **¼ tsp. salt**
- **¼ tsp. mustard powder**

2. Whisk together the lemon juice, olive oil, salt, and mustard powder. Mix into salad. Refrigerate and set aside for 1 to 24 hours.
3. Arrange a bed of escarole leaves on salad plates and add the salad.

Variation:

- Substitute brine-cured olives for the oil-cured olives and eliminate the salt.

Quinoa Taboule

Earthy, Middle Eastern taboule gains in flavor and texture when made with quinoa rather than the traditional bulgur. It also gains in nutrition and vitality as quinoa is a whole, rather than a refined, grain. Light and refreshing—yet substantial—taboule is the ideal summer salad.

Prep Tip: Prepare taboule from 1 to 2 days in advance. Cover well and refrigerate.

Yield: 2 servings
Prep Time: 5 minutes, using cooked quinoa
Total Time: 1 hour

Salad:

- **2 cups cooked, cooled quinoa**
- **1 cup chopped parsley**
- **½ cup chopped scallions**
- **2 Tbsp. chopped fresh mint (or 1 tsp. dried)**
- **1 garlic clove, minced or pressed**
- **1 Tbsp. minced fresh basil (½ tsp. dried)**
- **½ cup fresh lemon juice**

1. Toss together all salad ingredients except the lettuce. Chill for 1 hour or more to allow flavors to blend.
2. Line a salad bowl with lettuce leaves. Add taboule and garnish with olives and mint.

¼ cup extra virgin olive oil
¼ tsp. salt
⅛ tsp. freshly ground white pepper
red lettuce leaves

Garnish:
6 oil-cured olives
fresh mint

Quinoa in Herbed Yogurt Dressing on Lettuce Hearts

Iceberg lettuce has received more than its share of bad press for having a poor nutritional profile, but it is unsurpassed in the category of refreshing crispness. Here I use iceberg as an edible serving vessel for the wholesome ingredients of quinoa, herbs, and yogurt.

Yield: **2 servings**
Time: **15 minutes, using cooked quinoa**

Salad:
½ tsp. salt
1 Tbsp. fresh lime juice
1 Tbsp. minced fresh thyme leaves (½ tsp. dried)
¼ cup chopped parsley
¼ cup extra virgin olive oil
¼ cup yogurt
⅛ cup orange blossom honey
1 small head iceberg lettuce
1 cup cooked, cooled quinoa

Garnish:
sprigs of parsley or fresh thyme

1. Dissolve the salt in the lime juice. Place it with thyme, parsley, oil, yogurt, and honey in a blender. Blend until smooth.
2. Slice lettuce in half. Remove the center of each half and reserve for another use.
3. Combine the quinoa with the yogurt dressing. Divide between the two lettuce halves and garnish with sprigs of parsley or thyme.

Variations:
- Substitute tofu blended with oil and water for the yogurt.
- Substitute sour cream for the yogurt and use as a party dip.
- Vary herbs, using whatever fresh ones are available—lemon grass, oregano, tarragon, or dill weed.
- Substitute vinegar, lemon juice, or grapefuit juice for the lime juice.

Sweet Potato, Quinoa, and Chives

This sweetly piquant salad titillates the taste buds. Lightly cooked sweet potato will be a new taste experience for many; it enhances quinoa's distinct flavor and mâche's velvety texture. Halve the yield and serve as a spring luncheon entrée along with a light soup and fresh bread.

Prep Tip: Chill salad at least 1 hour prior to serving, and preferably overnight. Purchase only fresh mâche and use it immediately. For the best flavor, use a fresh, unbruised sweet potato and do not peel it.

Yield: 2 to 4 servings
Prep Time: 10 minutes, using cooked quinoa
Total Time: 70 minutes

Dressing:
2 Tbsp. white wine vinegar
1 Tbsp. roasted sesame oil
2 tsp. wildflower honey
1 tsp. natural soy sauce or tamari
½ tsp. grated fresh ginger

Salad:
1 small sweet potato, very finely diced (about 1 cup)
juice from ½ orange
1 cup cooked, cooled quinoa
½ cup thinly sliced chives
2 Tbsp. slivered almonds
1 small bunch mâche

1. Using a whisk, combine the dressing ingredients in a small bowl. Set aside.
2. Toss freshly cut sweet potato with the orange juice to prevent discoloration.
3. Steam diced sweet potato over boiling water until just tender, about 1 1/2 to 3 minutes. Plunge into cold water to stop the cooking. Blot dry.
4. Toss together the sweet potatoes, quinoa, chives, almonds, and 3 tablespoons of the dressing. Chill at least 1 hour.
5. Toss the mâche leaves with the remaining dressing and arrange on individual serving plates. Portion salad onto mâche.

Variation:
- Substitute yam or squash such as butternut, kabocha, or buttercup for the sweet potato.

Quinoa in Carrot Aspic

Molded salads get high ratings from most cooks because they look elegant and are easy to make. They also hold up well and preserve the ingredients they contain. The agar-agar supplies valuable minerals. This glistening orange aspic shows off quinoa's tiny ring-shaped embryo.

Prep Tips: When cooking at high altitudes, soften agar-agar in water for several hours prior to use, or allow additional cooking time for the agar to dissolve.

Yield: 4 servings
Prep Time: 30 minutes, using cooked quinoa
Total Time: 2 hours

1 medium carrot, diced (about 1 cup)
1 cup vegetable stock
⅛ cup agar-agar flakes

1. Peel the carrot and slice it into 1/2-inch cubes. Place in a saucepan with water, agar-agar, and salt. Bring to a boil, being careful to not let liquid boil over. Reduce heat, cover, and simmer over low heat for 15 minutes.
2. Meanwhile, using a vegetable peeler or garnishing tool, remove a few thin strips of peel from the cucumber and set aside.

few grains of salt
1 cucumber
½ cup cooked quinoa

Dressing:
fresh soy mayonnaise, page 106

3. Rinse a 4-cup mold with cold water. After the carrots have cooked for 10 minutes, remove 3 tablespoons of the hot carrot liquid and spoon it into the mold to coat the areas where you want to place the cucumber peel. Arrange the peel to make a pleasing decoration. Set mold aside. (Continue cooking carrots an additional 5 minutes.)
4. Place the quinoa in a mixing bowl. Purée the hot carrot mixture in a blender until very smooth, then pour it over the quinoa, stirring with a whisk until any lumps of quinoa are gone.
5. Carefully pour the hot, puréed carrot mixture into the mold. Do not disturb the cucumber peel design.
6. Allow to set at room temperature for 1 hour. Cover, and chill for 30 minutes or more.
7. Unmold the aspic by loosening the edges first with a knife and then inverting it onto a serving dish.
8. Peel and slice the remaining cucumber and use as a garnish along with dollops of fresh soy mayonnaise.

Tofu, Quinoa, and Dulse Salad

The savory combination of tofu, sweet white wine, and dulse is reminiscent of crabmeat. This is an ideal summertime lunch salad served with rice crackers or wheat wafers.

Yield: **4 small or 2 large salads**
Time: **15 minutes, using cooked quinoa**

1 10-oz. piece firm tofu
1 cup water
½ cup sweet white wine
2 Tbsp. white miso
1 cup cooked, cooled quinoa
½ cup dulse flakes
½ Tbsp. fresh minced dill weed (¼ tsp. dried)
1 medium cucumber, peeled, seeded, and diced
1 tsp. raspberry wine vinegar
2 Tbsp. mayonnaise

1. Dice the tofu into 1-inch squares and place in a saucepan with water, wine, and miso. Bring to a boil and simmer for 10 minutes. Drain, discarding the cooking water.
2. Mash the tofu in a food processor or with a potato masher. Stir in the quinoa, dulse, dill weed, cucumber, vinegar, and mayonnaise.
3. Divide the sprouts on serving plates. Top each with the tofu-quinoa mixture. Slice or dice the tomatoes and arrange them around the salads.

Variations:
- Substitute farmer's cheese or a combination of feta and ricotta cheeses for the tofu, and omit simmering in water, wine, and miso.
- Use the salad as a sandwich filling.

2 cups alfalfa sprouts
2 medium tomatoes

- Substitute oranges for the tomatoes, grapes for the cucumber, and honey for the dill weed. Omit the vinegar.
- Substitute homegrown quinoa sprouts for the alfalfa sprouts.

Marinated Black Beans, Quinoa, and Sweet Corn

This salad sparkles with clean colors and is packed with both nutrition and flavor. Serve it as a first course, a side dish, or as a summer meal.

Prep Tip: To cook black beans, place the beans, garlic, and twice the amount of water as beans in a crock pot and simmer 8 to 10 hours. Add 1/3 teaspoon salt per cup of dry measure beans, after they have softened. Pressure-cooking makes the beans too soft for salad presentations. Canned beans can be used, although they tend to be overly salty and lacking in vitality.

Yield: 2 large or 4 small servings
Prep Time: 45 minutes, using cooked black beans
Total Time: 3 hours, 45 minutes

Dressing:
¼ tsp. salt
1 Tbsp. fresh lemon juice
¼ cup extra virgin olive oil
2 Tbsp. minced parsley

Salad:
2 cups water
2 ears corn, husked
1 small carrot, diced small
¼ cup quinoa
¼ tsp. cumin seeds
½ cup cooked black beans
1 medium tomato, diced small
2 Tbsp. minced red onion
3 cups tender spinach leaves

1. Dissolve the salt in the lemon juice. Add the oil and parsley. Set aside.
2. Bring the water to a boil, add the corn, and cook over medium heat for 5 minutes. Remove corn. Simmer the diced carrot in the same water for 3 minutes. Drain the carrots, reserving 1/2 cup of this corn and carrot stock.
3. Bring the 1/2 cup of stock to a boil in a small saucepan. Add the quinoa and cumin. Cover, reduce heat, and cook over low heat for 20 minutes. Fluff with a fork and cool.
4. Place the beans in a strainer and rinse under cold water until all the "bean juice" is gone.
5. Remove the corn kernels from the cob. Combine with the quinoa, black beans, carrots, tomato, onion, and dressing. Stir well, then refrigerate for 3 hours or more, stirring occasionally to distribute the dressing. Serve on spinach greens.

Variations:

- Substitute quinoa pasta for the quinoa.
- Substitute fried tempeh, cranberry beans, or bolita beans for the black beans.
- Substitute sweet bell pepper for the carrot and add 2 tablespoons toasted sunflower seeds.

Sardine Antipasto

This Old-World dish reflects a return to sensible eating. A small amount of fish flavors the grain, which is surrounded by an abundance of fresh vegetables and savories. The flavors, colors, and textures work to satisfy all our appetites.

Yield: 2 servings
Time: 20 minutes, using cooked quinoa

12 string beans, tipped
6 to 8 leaves Boston or Bibb lettuce
1 cup cooked, cooled quinoa
1 small (3¾ oz.) tin of sardines packed in olive oil
1 cucumber, sliced
1 lemon, sliced
1 tomato, sliced
6 black olives
2 pepperoncini (pickled hot peppers)
1 carrot

1. Steam the string beans over boiling water until tender but still bright green, about 5 minutes. Plunge into cold water to cool.
2. Arrange washed and dried lettuce leaves on two plates. Fluff quinoa and pile 1/2 cup on each lettuce bed.
3. Lift sardines from the tin and divide between the two plates. Reserve olive oil.
4. Arrange the string beans, cucumber, lemon, tomato, olives, and pepperoncini on plates. Drizzle on olive oil.
5. Peel the carrot with a vegetable peeler. Remove a few strips of carrot by peeling lengthwise. Wrap these strips into tight curls and garnish the salads with them.

Variation:

- Any of the following can be added or substituted: raw Bermuda onion slices, feta cheese, marinated artichoke hearts, marinated mushrooms, anchovies, pickled garlic, steamed cauliflower, okra pickles, or pickled immature corn.

Chicken Salad with Quinoa, Grapes, and Cashews

This quickly assembled, substantial and well-balanced salad adds flair to any meal. For a sandwich, layer it with lettuce into a whole-wheat pita pocket bread. When entertaining, serve it in cream-puff shells.

Prep Tip: Make from 1 to 24 hours in advance.

Yield: 2 entrées or 4 side dishes
Prep Time: 5 minutes
Total Time: 1 hour

1. Combine the quinoa, chicken, grapes, cashews, and onion.
2. Whisk together the dressing ingredients and toss with the salad ingredients. Chill for 1 hour.

Salad:
- **4 cups cooked, cooled quinoa**
- **1 cup cooked chicken, cubed**
- **1 cup seedless red grapes, halved**
- **½ cup roasted cashews, halved**
- **1 medium red onion, chopped**
- **8 to 12 Romaine lettuce leaves**

Dressing:
- **⅓ cup extra virgin olive oil**
- **¼ cup champagne vinegar**
- **3 Tbsp. chopped fresh cilantro (1½ tsp. dried)**
- **½ tsp. salt**
- **¼ tsp. white pepper**

Garnish:
- **blood orange slices**
- **avocado slices**

Arrange on Romaine leaves and garnish with blood orange slices and avocado.

Variations:
- Substitute turkey or sautéed tofu cubes for the chicken.
- Substitute fresh currants for the grapes.

Cold Beef, Quinoa, and Watercress Salad

This easily made mélange blends robust flavors and vivid colors—it is perfect for an autumn Sunday supper and equally fitting for an elegant dinner party.

Prep Tip: For maximum flavor, use natural beef and marinate it 24 hours in advance.

Yield: 2 entrées or 4 side dishes
Prep Time: 10 minutes, using cooked beef
Total Time: 1 hour

Marinade:
- **2 Tbsp. balsamic vinegar**
- **2 Tbsp. Bordeaux wine**
- **1 clove garlic, minced or pressed**
- **1 tsp. natural soy sauce or tamari**
- **⅛ tsp. freshly ground black pepper**
- **½ cup extra virgin olive oil**

1. Whisk together marinade ingredients.
2. Toss the beef in the marinade and allow it to marinate for at least 1 hour.
3. Meanwhile, bring the water and pan juices to a boil, and add the quinoa, bay leaf, garlic, thyme, and salt. Cover and simmer for 20 minutes or until the liquid is absorbed. Remove from heat and allow to rest, covered, for 5 to 10 minutes. Fluff with a fork. Allow to cool.
4. Toss together the marinated beef, quinoa, and watercress. Place in a serving bowl or arrange in individual salad bowls.

Variations:
- Substitute game, poultry or seitan for the beef.
- Substitute arugula for the watercress.

Salad:

- ½ lb. cooked roast beef, cut into bite-sized pieces (about 1 cup)
- 2¾ cups water
- ¼ cup pan juices from roast beef
- 1½ cups quinoa
- 1 small bay leaf
- 1 clove garlic
- 1 Tbsp. minced fresh thyme (½ tsp. dried)
- pinch of salt
- 2 bunches of watercress, leaves cut coarsely, stems finely chopped (about 3 cups)

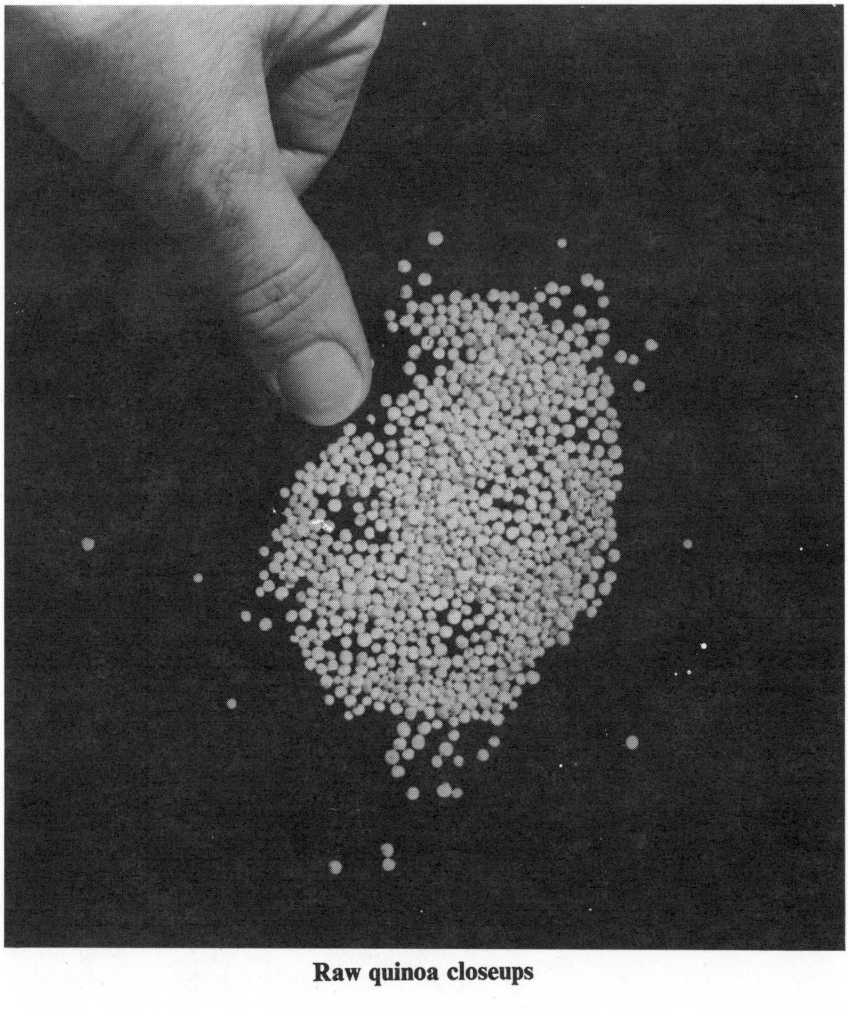

Raw quinoa closeups

13. Vegetarian Entrees

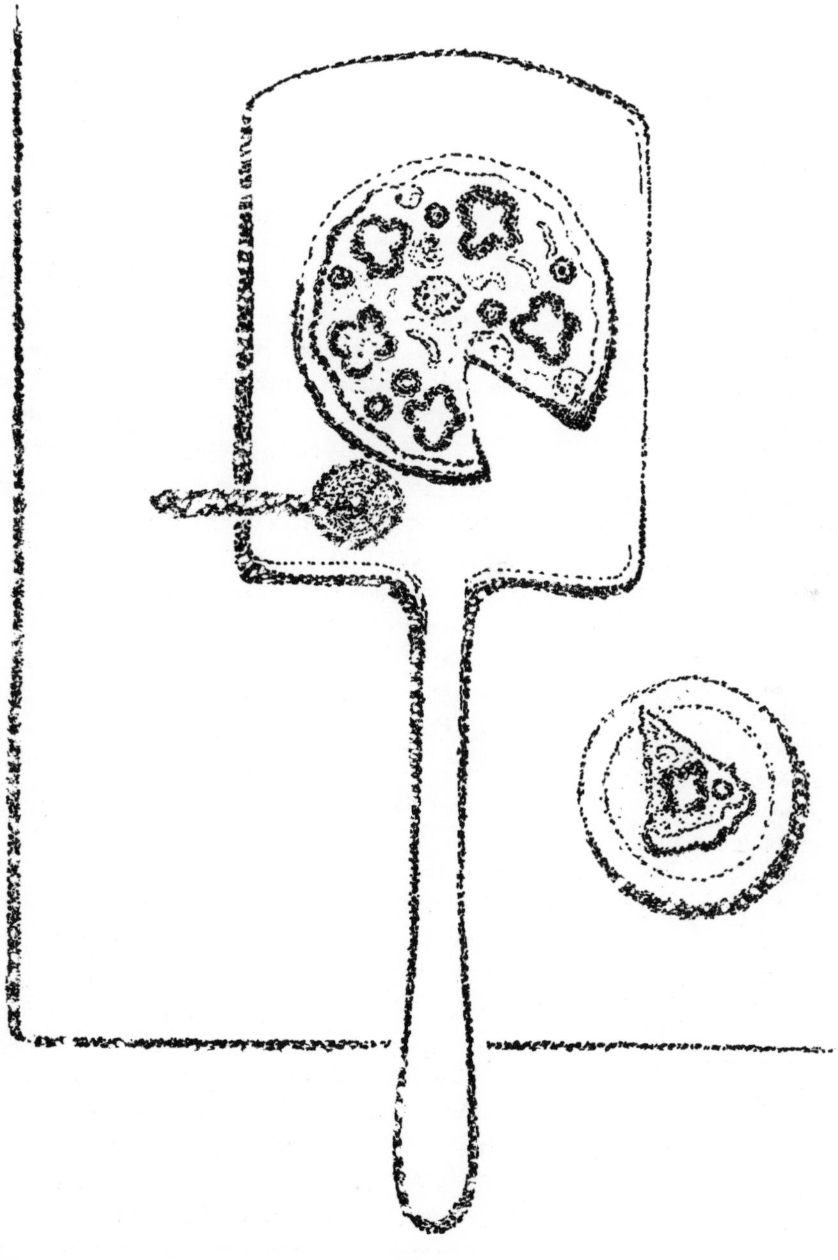

Fava, Quinoa, and Celeriac Ragout

The hearty—almost bitter—fava flavor looses its rough edges when combined with quinoa. Admittedly, fava beans require extra preparation time, but their melting texture and unusual flavor make them well worth the effort. For a simple meal, serve this ragout with a steamed leafy green or salad or as part of a Latin-style buffet or brunch.

Prep Tip: Soak fava beans to remove their outer shells. Like shucking peas, shelling these huge beans is a pleasant task—with or without company—unless you are rushed. The shelled beans and their seasonings may be cooked the day before the ragout is made.

Yield: 6 servings
Prep Time: 30 minutes
Total Time: 8 hours

Beans:
- **1 cup fava beans**
- **1 green Fresno chili, blistered, steamed, peeled, seeded and diced**
- **2 fresh tomatoes, chopped**
- **¼ tsp. turmeric**
- **1 tsp. cumin seeds**
- **2 cloves garlic, minced or pressed**
- **3 cups water**

Casserole:
- **1 Tbsp. unsalted butter**
- **1 onion, diced**
- **1 small celeriac, peeled and diced (about 1½ cups)**
- **1 cup quinoa**
- **1 cup vegetable stock**
- **½ tsp. salt**

Garnish:
- **parsley sprigs**

1. Soak the fava beans for 8 hours or until their tough outer skins soften.
2. After soaking, tear or cut off the skin tip from the base of the bean, then press the opposite end of the bean between thumb and forefinger to pop the bean out of its skin.
3. Place the shelled favas in a 2-quart pot with the chili, tomatoes, turmeric, cumin, garlic and water. Bring to a boil, cover, and simmer for 1 hour or until the beans are tender, adding more water during cooking, if necessary, to maintain liquid and ingredients at the same level.
4. In a small skillet melt the butter and sauté the onion, celeriac, and quinoa for 5 minutes or until the onion is tender.
5. Add the sautéed quinoa, stock, and salt to the fava beans. Cover and simmer for 20 minutes or until the liquid is absorbed and the grain is soft. Adjust seasonings. Garnish with parsley. For the best flavor, do not serve piping hot.

Variations:
- Substitute lima beans, tofu, or seitan for the fava.
- Fill a vegetable potpie with the ragout.
- Serve atop whole wheat chapati with a dollop of plain yogurt.
- Substitute 1 Tbsp. light miso for a portion of the salt. To do this, cook 1/4 tsp. salt into the softened beans for 10 minutes, purée miso with stock and add it to the quinoa-bean mixture during the last minute of cooking.

See Glossary for descriptions of unfamiliar ingredients. See Appendix for information on quinoa flour, chilies and natural sugar.

Curried Quinoa and Pistachio Pilaf

Curried quinoa is a welcome change to an otherwise traditional East Indian rice dish. A stock made from leek rootlets, pea pods, or corn cobs, borage, and kombu seaweed amplifies the flavors.

Prep Tip: I do not recommend buying pistachios already shelled because once out of the shell, the nuts quickly become rancid. Shelling them yourself is surprisingly easy when you use the method described in step 2 below.

Yield: 6 servings
Time: 30 minutes

4 cups vegetable stock
2 cups quinoa
½ tsp. salt
1 cup unsalted pistachio nuts in shell
2 tsp. ghee
3 shallots, diced
1 small onion, diced
1 large carrot, diced
1 Tbsp. garam masala
2 tsp. ground coriander
1 tsp. cumin seeds
½ tsp. turmeric
½ cup raisins

1. Bring the stock to a boil in a 2 1/2-quart pot. Add the salt and quinoa, cover, and simmer for 20 minutes or until the liquid is absorbed.
2. Meanwhile, shell the pistachio nuts by holding each one on a cutting board between thumb and foreigner. Place knife blade where shell splits and slice down to open. Reserve 30 nut halves for garnish and coarsely chop the remaining nuts. Set aside.
3. Place the ghee in a wok or skillet and sauté the shallots, onion, and carrots for 3 to 5 minutes or until limp. Stir in the garam masala, coriander, cumin, turmeric, raisins, and chopped pistachios. Cook for 2 to 3 minutes. Set aside.
4. When the quinoa is cooked, remove from heat and allow to rest, covered, for 5 to 10 minutes, then fluff with a fork.
5. Fold the curried vegetables into the quinoa. Heat, stirring gently—or bake, covered—until heated through. Garnish with the remaining pistachios.

Variations:

- Use cooked pilaf as a stuffing for eggplant or zucchini. Stuff the partially baked vegetable(s) and return to the oven for the last 15 minutes of baking.
- Substitute roasted cashews for pistachios. Substitute sesame oil for ghee.

Wehani Quinoa Pilaf

Serve this versatile red-rice pilaf next to or under vegetables or meat, or stuffed into winter squash or poultry. The smoothness of the quinoa compliments Wehani's nutty flavor. While cooking, this rice fills the kitchen with an aroma like that of fresh buttered popcorn.

Prep Tip: This pilaf is foolproof, especially when made with the help of a timer. Set the timer to ring after the rice has simmered 25 minutes. After it rings, add the quinoa.

Yield: 4 servings
Prep Time: 10 minutes, using prepared chicken stock
Total Time: 1 hour

2 Tbsp. unsalted butter
1 medium onion, diced small
2 medium celery ribs with leaves, diced small
1 Tbsp. fresh minced rosemary (or ½ tsp. dried)
½ cup Wehani rice
1¾ cups unsalted chicken or turkey stock
¼ cup sauterne
1 Tbsp. natural soy sauce or tamari
½ cup quinoa

1. Heat a large skillet over medium heat, add butter, and sauté onions and then celery for about 5 minutes or until they become limp. Add rosemary and stir for an additional minute.
2. Push the onion and celery mixture to the side of the pan, add Wehani rice, and sauté over medium heat for about 3 minutes.
3. Add the stock, wine, and soy sauce. Bring to a boil, reduce heat, cover, and simmer for 25 minutes.
4. Add the quinoa and simmer for an additional 20 minutes or until the liquid is absorbed. Remove from heat and allow to set, covered, for 5 to 10 minutes. Fluff with a fork.

Variations:

- Substitute wild rice for the Wehani rice.
- Substitute a Granny Smith apple and thyme for the celery and rosemary.
- Add currants and pine nuts, wrap in grape leaves, and bake with a lemon juice marinade.

Chilean Quinoa Pilaf

The Bistro, located on an old Spanish land grant called the Baca (adjacent to Crestone, Colorado), happens to be in the heart of quinoa-growing country. Bistro Chef Suzanne Foote often features this quinoa pilaf on the menu. It has a lively and authentic Chilean flavor—authentic but for the anasazi, bean substitute, a favorite bean of the Four Corners region. In Chile, the typical bean is the *tarwi.*

Yield: 6
Time: 30 minutes, using cooked anasazi

1 tsp. unsalted butter
1 clove garlic, minced or pressed
3 shallots, diced
1 onion, diced
1 jalapeño chili, blistered, steamed, peeled, seeded, and diced
1½ cups quinoa
1 Tbsp. red pepper flakes
1 tsp. cumin seeds
¼ tsp. salt
⅛ tsp. freshly ground black pepper
3 cups vegetable stock
1 cup cooked anasazi beans

1. In a 2-quart pot, heat the butter and briefly sauté the garlic, shallots, onion, chili and quinoa. Add seasonings and sauté one additional minute.
2. Add the stock and anasazi, bring to a boil, reduce heat, cover, and simmer for 20 minutes or until the liquid is absorbed. Mix ingredients gently but thoroughly from top to bottom and spoon into a serving bowl.

Variations:

- Prepare extra and reserve 2 cups for the Zapallo and Quinoa Casserole (see following recipe).
- Add 1 cup sweet corn kernels.
- Serve chilled on lettuce with a creamy avocado dressing.
- Substitute seitan or pinto beans for the anasazi.

Zapallo and Quinoa Casserole

This zesty casserole combines a spicy jalapeño, quinoa, and anasazi pilaf with the sweet squash, zapallo. Slabs of the enormous and vividly orange-fleshed zapallo are omnipresent in South American food markets; some are so large that they fill a hand cart. Also called calabaza, or West Indian pumpkin, zapallos can be found in specialty markets, and you will be seeing them in more produce departments. If zapallo is not available, substitute an orange-fleshed winter squash.

Prep Tip: Prepare Chilean Quinoa Pilaf (see preceding recipe) up to one day in advance.

Yield: 4 to 6 servings
Prep Time: 30 minutes, using cooked Chilean Quinoa Pilaf
Total Time: 1 ½ hours

Casserole:
2 cups zapallo squash
⅛ tsp. salt
2 cups Chilean Quinoa Pilaf (see recipe above)
½ cup bread crumbs

1. Preheat oven to 350°F.
2. Remove seeds from the squash, cut into chunks, sprinkle with the salt, and steam over boiling water until tender, about 10 minutes.
3. Meanwhile, melt the butter over low heat. Add the flour and salt. Stir for 3 minutes. Remove from heat and allow to cool. Slowly stir in the milk. Return to heat. Cook and stir the roux with a wire whisk until thickened and smooth, about 3 to 5 minutes.
4. Oil an 8 by 8-inch casserole. Add bread crumbs and shake to form an even coating on the oiled surface.

Quinoa Roux:
- **2 Tbsp. unsalted butter**
- **3 Tbsp. quinoa flour**
- **1/8 tsp. salt**
- **1 cup milk or vegetable stock**

Garnish:
- **1 Tbsp. minced fresh cilantro**

5. Remove the skin from the squash. Purée squash in a food processor or blender and spread into the prepared casserole. Spread a layer of Chilean Quinoa Pilaf over the squash.
6. Top the casserole with the roux and bake in a preheated oven for 20 minutes or until the top is browned. Garnish individual servings with cilantro.

Variations:
- Substitute slices of Jack cheese for the roux.
- Substitute Wehani Rice Pilaf for the Chilean Quinoa Pilaf.

Skillet Pizza with Brie and Asparagus in Quinoa Biscuit Crust

A novel interpretation of an old theme, this pizza satisfies a hunger for beauty as well as for good food. Its rich buttermilk-and-quinoa crust has little in common with the usual yeasted version.

Prep Tip: Refrigerate the brie to make slicing easier.

Yield: 1 10-inch pizza
Prep Time: 25 minutes
Total Time: 45 minutes

Crust:
- **1 cup quinoa flour**
- **1 tsp. baking soda**
- **1/2 tsp. salt**
- **1/2 cup unbleached white flour**
- **3 Tbsp. unsalted butter, chilled**
- **1/3 cup buttermilk**

Filling:
- **8 plum tomatoes**
- **1/4 tsp. salt**
- **8 asparagus spears**
- **6 to 8 pearl onions**
- **4 to 6 medium mushrooms**
- **1/4 lb. Brie cheese**
- **1/4 lb. mozzarella**
- **1 Tbsp. minced fresh oregano (or 1/2 tsp. dried)**
- **1 Tbsp. extra virgin olive oil**

1. In a food processor, combine the quinoa flour, soda salt, and 1/4 cup of the white flour. Add the butter and process until blended. Add the buttermilk and process until dough forms a ball. Set aside.
2. Dice the tomatoes, toss with the salt, and set in a strainer to drain.
3. Break tough stem ends off asparagus. Peel and discard tough outer layers from these ends. Steam peeled ends, together with the tender tips, over boiling water for 5 minutes. Slice into 1/2-inch pieces and set aside.
4. Slice the onions very thin. Remove the stems from the mushrooms and discard. Slice the caps very thin. Grate mozzarella. Slice Brie into strips.
5. Preheat oven to 375°F.
6. Roll dough out to an 11-inch circle on a surface floured with the remaining 1/4 cup of white flour. Slide dough circle into a buttered 10-inch cast-iron skillet. Press edges all around to form a 1/2-inch rim.
7. Sprinkle the mozzarella over the crust. Press remaining liquid from the tomatoes and lay half of

them on top of the mozzarella. On top of the tomatoes, layer the onions, mushrooms, Brie, aspragus, and finally, the remaining tomatoes. Sprinkle with oregano and drizzle with olive oil. Bake for 20 minutes.

Variations:

- Substitute raw, slivered green peppers, cooked artichoke hearts, or thin zucchini slices for the asparagus.
- Roll dough out to a thickness of 1/4 inch, cut with a floured biscuit cutter, and bake for 15 minutes as biscuits.
- Substitute chopped green chili for mushrooms.
- Substitute Feta cheese for Brie.

Shiitake Quinoa Pie in Crimson Crust

This stunning crimson-orange crust shares equal billing with the rich and complex filling. Garnet yam yields the most dramatic color, but if it is unavailable, use Jersey sweet potato or orange-fleshed winter squash. This pie is surprisingly easy to prepare.

Prep Tip: The 3 cups cooked quinoa and/or yam may be prepared the day before. If dried shiitake are used, soak in water for 2 to 8 hours prior to slicing.

Yield: 1 9-inch pie
Time: 50 minutes

Crust:

- **1 cup quinoa flour**
- **½ tsp. salt**
- **¼ cup unsalted butter**
- **1 small garnet yam, peeled, sliced into 1-inch cubes (1 cup)**
- **1 cup cooked wild rice and quinoa**
- **1 egg, well beaten**

Filling:

- **1 Tbsp. unsalted butter**
- **2 shallots, minced**
- **½ cup sliced shiitake mushrooms, fresh or dried and soaked**
- **⅓ cup diced red bell pepper**

1. Preheat oven to 400°F. Oil an 8-inch pie pan.
2. Steam yam for about 5 minutes or just until tender. Plunge into cold water to cool and then set aside.
3. In a food processor, combine the quinoa flour with the salt. Add the butter, yam, and egg and process just until dough forms a ball. Using your fingers, press into an oiled pie pan. Bake for 15 minutes. Remove pie from oven and reduce heat to 350°F.
4. While the crust is baking, heat a frying pan and add butter. Briefly sauté the shallots, shiitake, pepper, and watercress. Add the mirin and soy sauce.
5. Blend the sautéed vegetables with the quinoa and 3/4 cup of the cheese. Spread onto the prepared crust. Sprinkle the remaining 1/4 cup cheese on top and bake at 350°F. for 20 minutes or until the bottom and edges are golden.

1 cup chopped watercress
2 Tbsp. mirin
1 tsp. natural soy sauce or tamari
2 cups cooked wild rice and quinoa
1 cup Fontina cheese, grated

Variations:
- Fill pie crust with quiche or shepherd's pie fillings.
- Substitute Gruyere, havarti, Muenster or Swiss cheese for the Fontina.
- Substitute sweet sherry for the mirin.

Stuffed Green Peppers in Yellow Pepper Sauce

The sauce on these green peppers looks like melted cheese but is actually a light and unusual purée of sweet peppers. Inside the green peppers another surprise awaits—a duo of smokey cheese and quinoa.

Yield: 4 servings
Prep Time: 30 minutes
Total Time: 1 ½ hours

Filling:
1 cup water
½ cup dry white wine
⅛ tsp. salt
1 Tbsp. minced fresh tarragon (½ tsp. dried)
¾ cup quinoa
¾ cup grated smoked cheese (Edam, Gouda, Swiss)
¾ cup ricotta cheese

Sauce:
6 yellow bell peppers, blistered, steamed, peeled, and seeded
1 tsp. salt

Peppers:
8 green bell peppers

1. Preheat oven to 350°F.
2. In a saucepan, bring to a boil the water, wine, salt, and tarragon. Add the quinoa, cover, reduce heat, and cook over low heat for 20 minutes. When cooked, remove from heat and allow to rest, covered, for 5 to 10 minutes. Fluff with fork.
3. Meanwhile, place the yellow peppers and salt in a processor or blender and purée until smooth.
4. Combine the cooked quinoa with the cheeses. Slice the green peppers into halves from top to bottom and remove seeds and stems. Fill each with quinoa-cheese mixture and arrange in an oiled baking dish.
5. Pour the yellow pepper sauce over the stuffed peppers. Cover with foil and bake for 1 hour. Spoon the sauce that is in the pan over peppers before serving.

Variations:
- Substitute red bell peppers for the yellow peppers.
- Substitute seasoned tofu for the cheeses.
- Substitute fresh basil for tarragon and mozzarella cheese for the smoked cheese: cover with a light tomato sauce rather than the yellow pepper sauce.

Quinoa, Chili, and Cheddar Cheese in Potato Skin

Every busy cook needs a collection of recipes like the following—a dish that almost makes itself while the cook is busy with other preparations.

Prep Tip: A stuffed potato will wait in a warm oven for an hour with no complaints.

Yield: 1 serving
Prep Time: 10 minutes, using cooked quinoa
Time: 1 hour

1 large russet potato
$\frac{1}{4}$ cup cooked quinoa
1 Tbsp. green chili, blistered, steamed, peeled, seeded, and chopped
$\frac{1}{4}$ cup grated sharp cheddar cheese

Garnish:
paprika

1. Pre-heat oven to 400°F.
2. Bake the potato for 45 minutes, or until it is tender throughout.
3. Slash the top and scoop out the cooked potato. While still hot, mix it with quinoa, chili, and cheese. Restuff potato. Garnish with paprika.

Variations:
- Substitute minced bell pepper (red, yellow, or green) for the green chili.
- Add corn kernels.
- Vary the cheese or combine with Monterey Jack, Swiss, or mozzarella.

Quinoa, Walnuts, and Herbs Baked in Tomato Halves

Because the tomatoes are highly seasoned and baked alone first, they do not really flavor the walnut-quinoa filling. The filling maintains its own pleasant identity in this Mediterranean-inspired dish. Leftovers make good cold appetizers the next day. Or, reheat them and serve as a side dish to a creamy pasta entrée.

Yield: 4 servings
Time: 1 hour, using cooked quinoa

Tomatoes:
4 medium tomatoes
$\frac{1}{2}$ tsp. salt
1 Tbsp. minced fresh rosemary (or $\frac{1}{2}$ tsp. dried)
1 Tbsp. fresh minced basil (or $\frac{1}{2}$ tsp. dried)

1. Preheat oven to 350°F.
2. Slice the tomatoes in half crosswise. Using a melon baller, scoop out the seeds and center pulp. Sprinkle with the salt, and invert on a rack to drain for 20 minutes.
3. Roast walnuts in the oven for 7 to 10 minutes, watching carefully at the end so they do not burn. Chop very fine and mix well with quinoa and miso.
4. In a small mixing bowl, combine the herbs and oil.
5. Place the drained tomatoes in an oiled, oven-proof serving dish. Spoon the oil and herb mixture

1 Tbsp. fresh minced marjoram (or ½ tsp. dried)
2 Tbsp. extra virgin olive oil

Filling:
½ cup walnuts
1½ cups cooked quinoa
2 Tbsp. sweet white miso
¼ cup dry red wine

Garnish:
minced parsley

onto them. Using a spoon, distribute the herbs over the insides and cut edges of the tomatoes. Bake, uncovered, for 10 minutes.
6. Fill the tomatoes with the quinoa mixture. Spoon 1/2 tablespoon of the red wine over each tomato filling. Return to the oven and bake for an additional 10 minutes. Set dish under broiler and broil for 5 minutes or until the tops are lightly browned.

Variations:
- Substitute pumpkin seeds for the walnuts.
- Substitute baby eggplant for the tomatoes.
- Substitute pine nuts for the walnuts and Parmesan cheese for the miso, triple the amount of basil, and eliminate the other herbs.

Chinese Greens with Peanut Quinoa

Quinoa forms the background for this characteristically intriguing collection of Oriental tastes and textures.

Prep Tip: Have all ingredients sliced and at hand before heating the oil. If you are cooking quinoa fresh, omit stir-frying. Place it in a separate serving bowl and use it as a base for the stir-fried vegetables.

Yield: 4 servings
Time: 30 minutes

1½ cups broccoli florets
1 tsp. ginger juice
3 Tbsp. peanut oil
4 leaves bok choy, sliced into 1-inch pieces
4 leaves Chinese cabbage, sliced into 1-inch pieces
½ tsp. salt
1 bunch scallions, sliced into 1-inch pieces
3 cloves garlic, minced or pressed
12 snow peas, stems removed
2 Tbsp. natural soy sauce or tamari
1 cup cooked quinoa
¼ cup dry-roasted peanuts

1. Steam the broccoli florets over boiling water until they are tender but still bright green, about 5 minutes.
2. Heat a large skillet or wok. Add the oil, and when it is hot (but not smoking), add the bok choy, Chinese cabbage, and salt. Continue to stir over medium to high heat for about 3 minutes. Add the scallions, garlic, and snow peas. Continue to stir until greens are limp.
3. Add the broccoli florets, ginger juice, and soy sauce. Finally, add the quinoa and peanuts. Heat through and serve.

Variations:
- Alternative vegetables include: broccoli rabe, celery, garden peas, celery cabbage, onions, water chestnuts, and mung-bean sprouts.
- Substitute toasted sesame oil for the peanut oil; add a dash of hot pepper seame oil.

Quinoa Chilies Rellenos Con Queso

Cheese-stuffed chilies (*chiles rellenos con queso*) are a classic Mexican dish. Replace the typical *rellenos* batter of wheat flour with versatile quinoa, and the result is exciting. The crisp quinoa covering hides a tender, piquant layer of green chili, which in turn surrounds the melted Camembert. And they are beautiful to look at because deep-frying colors quinoa golden and emphasizes its distinctive beady texture.

Prep Tip: To be sure that oil is sufficiently hot for deep-frying, check it with a food thermometer or test it by adding a few drops of batter. The batter bits should sink to the bottom and almost immediately rise to the surface.

Yield: 4 servings
Time: 20 minutes, using cooked quinoa and prepared chilies

peanut oil for deep-frying
4 oz. Camembert cheese
4 poblano chilies, blistered, steamed, peeled, slashed along one side, and seeded
1 egg, slightly beaten
2 cups cooked, cooled quinoa

1. Preheat oil to 375°F.
2. Slice the cheese into strips that will fit into chilies. Stuff chilies with cheese.
3. Combine the egg and the quinoa. Place 1/4 cup of the mixture in the palm of one hand, lay a stuffed chili on top, and cover with another 1/4 cup of the quinoa mixture. Using both hands, pat and press the quinoa covering to enclose the chili.
4. Gently slide each assembled chili into the preheated oil and deep-fry until golden brown and crisp. Drain and serve hot.

Variations:

- Substitute 3 ounces of Fontina and 1 ounce of Gorgonzola cheese for the Camembert.
- Use the same quinoa batter for deep-frying shrimp, fish strips, or vegetables such as thinly sliced carrots, onions, green pepper, summer squash, yams, or whole mushrooms.

Sweet and Sour Quinoa Tempeh

There is nothing boring about this exotic dish, which successfully borrows from several culinary traditions. Serve it with mild background food like basmati rice or pasta.

Prep Tip: The complex flavors of this recipe blend more fully if the dish is prepared a day or two before it is served. Chill and reheat it prior to serving.

Yield: 2 to 3 servings
Time: 45 minutes

6 Tbsp. sesame oil
2 Tbsp. coriander seeds
1 10-oz. package quinoa tempeh, diced into ½-inch squares
4 to 5 cloves garlic, minced or pressed
1 cup finely diced pineapple
6 Tbsp. tomato paste
½ cup water
3 Tbsp. red wine vinegar
2 Tbsp. orange zest
1 tsp. salt

1. Heat a skillet or heavy pot. Add the oil and toast the coriander seeds over medium heat for 1 minute.
2. Add the tempeh and sauté for 5 minutes, stirring to brown it on all sides. Add the garlic, and sauté briefly, being careful not to let it brown.
3. Combine the pineapple, tomato paste, water, vinegar, orange zest and salt. Add to the tempeh, stir, cover, reduce heat, and simmer for 20 minutes.

Variation:
- Purée in a food processor and serve as a dip with crackers or vegetables, or as a sandwich spread.

Quinoa Spirals with Sun-Dried Tomatoes

A variety of quinoa pasta shapes (and ingredients) are available to expand your pasta repertoire and bestow an honest, whole-grain flavor on many different dishes. For this recipe, I prefer the spirals. Both the tomatoes and the zucchini retain their bright colors, resulting in a sparkling California-style dish.

Prep Tip: Allow extra cooking time for whole grain pastas and pay extra attention to prevent overcooking which results in soggy, broken pasta. As with white pasta, quinoa pasta is best when prepared "al dente."

Yield: 2 portions
Time: 45 minutes

3 qts. water
1 tsp. salt
12 oz. quinoa spirals
8 sun-dried tomato halves, dry packed
½ cup water
¼ tsp. salt
2 Tbsp. extra virgin olive oil
3 cloves garlic, minced or pressed
1 medium zucchini, grated
2 Tbsp. pine nuts

1. Bring 3 quarts water and salt to a boil. Add the spirals, stir, and cook for 15 minutes or until done.
2. Meanwhile, place the tomato halves in 1/2 cup water with 1/4 teaspoon salt. Bring to a boil, cover, and simmer over low heat for 15 minutes or until the water is absorbed. Dice and set aside.
3. Heat a large skillet or wok. Add the oil and sauté garlic briefly over low heat, being careful not to brown it. Add the zucchini and pine nuts. Stir for 2 minutes over medium heat. Add the tomatoes and pasta and continue to stir over medium heat for an additional 2 minutes.

Variations:
- Substitute walnuts for the pine nuts and add chopped fresh basil and grated Parmesan cheese.
- Substitute artichoke hearts for the grated zucchini.

14. Entrees Con Carne

Quinoa Jambalaya

If you want whole grain goodness in an authentic, flavorful, southern Louisiana jambalaya, choose quinoa as an ingredient. The quinoa and vegetables finish cooking at the same time (this would not be the case with brown rice).

Prep Tip: Use fully ripened tomatoes, as their juice provides necessary liquid for this dish.

Yield: 2 to 4
Time: 30 minutes

1 Tbsp. hot pepper sesame oil
1 Tbsp. quinoa flour
1 medium onion, diced
1 clove garlic, minced or pressed
2 large ripe tomatoes, diced
10 baby okra, sliced into ½-inch rounds
1 bay leaf
4 sprigs fresh thyme (or ½ tsp. dried)
½ tsp. salt
¾ cup fish stock
1 cup quinoa
1 medium bell pepper, chopped
½ cup chopped parsley
½ lb. medium shrimp, shelled and deveined
few dashes of natural hot pepper sauce or Tabasco

Garnish:
6 chives, finely chopped

1. Heat the oil in a heavy 2-quart saucepan suitable for table-service. Sauté the flour until a fragrant aroma is released, about 3 minutes. Add and sauté together for 5 minutes: the onion, garlic, tomatoes, okra, bay leaf, thyme, and salt. Cover and simmer for 10 minutes.
2. Add the stock, quinoa, pepper, and parsley, and bring to a boil. Reduce heat, cover, and simmer 15 minutes.
3. Arrange the shrimp on top of the quinoa and vegetables, and season with hot pepper sauce. Cover and simmer until the shrimp are cooked, about 5 to 7 minutes. Remove from heat and let rest 5 to 10 minutes. Fluff with a fork and garnish with chives.

Variations:
- Substitute langouste (spring rock lobster), game, poultry, or fried tempeh for the shrimp.
- Substitute 1 teaspoon red pepper flakes and unsalted butter for the hot pepper sesame oil.
- Add snow peas and water chestnuts when the shrimp are added. Eliminate the bell pepper and okra.

Oysters, Tomatoes, and Corn on Fried Quinoa Slices

Depending on how this entrée is presented, it can serve as a hearty fisherman's lunch or as the centerpiece of an elegant dinner party. The full-bodied, basil-spiked sauce of succulent oysters, tomatoes, and sweet corn perfectly complements the crisp quinoa slices.

Prep Tip: For a quick sauce, use canned oysters, frozen cut corn, and canned, chopped tomatoes.

See Glossary for descriptions of unfamiliar ingredients.
See Appendix for information on quinoa flour, chilies and natural sugar.

Yield: 4 servings
Prep Time: 30 minutes
Total Time: 2 hours

Quinoa slices:
- 2 cups water
- 1/8 tsp. salt
- 1 cup quinoa
- safflower oil for shallow pan-frying

Sauce:
- 8 medium tomatoes
- 1/4 tsp. salt
- kernels cut from 4 ears of corn
- 1 dozen oysters, fresh-shucked, in juice
- 1/4 cup fresh basil, coarsely chopped

1. Bring the water with the salt to a boil, add the quinoa, reduce heat, cover, and cook over low heat for 20 minutes.
2. Press the hot, cooked quinoa into a glass bread pan, let cool for 30 minutes at room temperature, cover, and chill in the refrigerator for 1 hour or more.
3. Add the tomatoes to boiling water to cover. Simmer for 5 minutes, drain, cool, peel, and remove seeds. Purée with the salt in a blender, food mill, or food processor.
4. Drain the oysters and reserve liquid. Place the tomatoes in a saucepan with the corn kernels and oyster liquid and cook over medium heat until excess liquid cooks away and corn is tender. Stir in the basil and whole oysters. Correct the seasoning. Cook over low heat for 5 minutes. Set sauce aside and keep warm.
5. Using a broad, sharp knife, cut the quinoa into 8 slices. Heat a large skillet over medium heat and add the oil. When the oil is hot, carefully place slices of quinoa in the pan. Pan-fry until golden brown and crisp, 2 to 4 minutes on each side. Place fried slices on serving dishes and spoon oyster sauce over each serving.

Variations:
- Substitute other shellfish or cooked white beans for the oysters.
- Substitute creamed vegetable sauce, picante sauce, a sweet-and-sour clear vegetable sauce, tomato sauce, or maple syrup for the oyster sauce.

Clams, Quinoa, and Parsley on Rigatoni

The classic combination of clams, garlic, parsley (a generous amount of it in this case), and pasta welcomes quinoa as a new ingredient. The quinoa also holds its own in this mix of assertive flavors. Serve with broiled tomatoes.

Yield: 4 servings
Time: 45 minutes

1. Bring the water and salt to a boil. Add the rigatoni, stir, and cook until tender but still firm to the bite. Drain.

5 qts. water
1 tsp. salt
12 oz. rigatoni (about 2 cups)
10 to 12 oz. clams in liquid
½ cup quinoa
2 Tbsp. extra virgin olive oil
2 cups minced parsley
4 to 6 cloves garlic, minced or pressed
1 Tbsp. minced fresh oregano (or ½ tsp. dried)

2. Meanwhile, drain the clams, reserving liquid. Measure the clam liquid and add water to make 1 cup stock. Bring stock to a boil. Add the quinoa, reduce heat, cover, and cook over low heat for 20 minutes. Mince the clams.
3. Heat a wok or skillet over medium heat. Add the oil and when it is hot, add the parsley, garlic, and oregano. Stir-fry for about 1 minute, add the clams, and continue stirring for another minute. Add the quinoa and pasta, and stir. Correct the seasonings and heat through.

Variations:
- Prepare the dish in advance and place in an ovenproof serving dish. Top with grated Parmesan cheese mixed with additional parsley and oregano. Heat covered at serving time.
- Substitute mussel, oysters, shrimp, or scallops for the clams.
- Substitute steamed vegetables such as carrots, cauliflower, sugar snap peas, mushrooms and/or tomatoes for clams.

Stir-fried Quinoa, Shrimp, and Water Chestnuts

Authentic Japanese seasonings and crisp vegetables blend with quinoa for an unmistakably Oriental "fried rice" dish. Quinoa offers the lightness of white rice and a more distinctive flavor and superior nutritional profile than either brown or white rice.

Serves 4
Time: 15 minutes, using cooked quinoa

2 Tbsp. roasted sesame oil
1 tsp. juice of freshly grated ginger
1 medium onion, diced
3 celery ribs and leaves, chopped
1 cup snow peas, sliced into ½-inch diagonals
½ cup sliced water chestnuts
4 cups quinoa, cooked
⅔ cup tiny shrimp, cooked
3 Tbsp. natural soy sauce or tamari

Heat the oil and ginger juice in a wok and sauté in the following order: onion, celery, snow peas, and water chestnuts. Mix in quinoa, shrimp, soy sauce, and saké. Cover and cook for 5 minutes or until the celery and peas are tender but still vibrantly green. Garnish. Serve hot.

Variations:
- Substitute fresh green beans or peas for the snow peas.
- Substitute chicken, tofu, cooked tempeh, or seitan for the shrimp.

1 Tbsp. saké or mirin

Garnish:
1 Tbsp. nori seaweed flakes

Lobster, Leeks, and Daikon with Cream Sauce in Quinoa Ring

Leeks and pungent daikon enhance the lobster's sweetness and the quinoa's piquancy. The shapes and colors of the ingredients add up to a visual feast that is matched by a fascinating play of flavors.

Yield: 2 to 4 servings
Time: 45 minutes

2 cups water
½ tsp. natural soy sauce or tamari
1 cup quinoa
⅓ cup chopped chives
2 Tbsp. unsalted butter
1 small leek, sliced (about 1 cup)
1 small daikon, sliced into ½-inch rounds, then quartered (about 1 cup)
⅛ tsp. salt
2 shallots, minced fine
2 large cloves garlic, minced or pressed
½ lb. cooked lobster meat, cut into bite-sized pieces
¼ cup dry white wine
1 Tbsp. minced fresh thyme (½ tsp. dried)
⅛ tsp. cayenne pepper
1 cup half-and-half cream

Garnish:
1 bunch watercress, cut into 2-inch lengths

1. Bring the water to a boil, add the soy sauce and quinoa. Cover and simmer for 20 minutes or until the liquid is absorbed. Remove from heat and allow to stand for 5 minutes. Stir in chopped chives. Cast into an oiled ring mold, press down, and set aside.
2. Melt 1 tablespoon of the butter in a large, heavy skillet. Briefly sauté the leeks and daikon. Add the salt, cover, and cook for about 20 minutes, or until the daikon is translucent. Stir as necessary. Transfer to a bowl.
3. Melt the remaining tablespoon of butter in the same skillet. Sauté the shallots and garlic. Stir in the lobster and wine and simmer until the lobster is heated through, about 3 minutes. Add the lobster to the leeks and daikon, using a slotted spoon.
4. To the skillet juices, mix in the thyme and cayenne. Strain any liquid from the lobster-leek mixture and add it to the skillet. Simmer until all liquid is reduced by half. Add the cream and simmer until slightly thickened, about 3 minutes. Stir in the lobster mixture and heat through. Adjust seasonings.
5. With a butter knife, loosen the quinoa from the mold. Position the ring on a serving plate. Using a slotted spoon, mound the lobster mixture in the center of the ring. Top with more of the sauce; garnish with watercress.

Variations:
- Color the sauce with annato or saffron.
- Substitute scallops for the lobster.

Trout and Quinoa Seviche

Really fresh fish deserves to be treated so that its delicate flavor can be appreciated. Seviche does this with élan. Even those who are reluctant to try sushi will enjoy fish "cooked" in citrus juice. Find the freshest trout available and fillet and skin it just before preparing.

Yield: 4 servings
Prep Time: 30 minutes
Total Time: 4 hours

Fish:
2 medium-sized whole trout
½ cup fresh lime juice
½ tsp. salt

Sauce:
6 tomatillos
1 cup cooked quinoa
2 medium tomatoes, diced small
1 small red onion, minced
2 Tbsp. red pepper flakes
1 Tbsp. coarsely cracked black peppercorns
½ cup minced cilantro
4 to 8 green lettuce leaves

1. Remove the head, tail, fins, bones, and skin from the trout. Slice into bite-sized pieces and place in a shallow glass dish.
2. Combine the lime juice and salt. Pour over fish, cover, and refrigerate for 3 to 8 hours.
3. Remove papery husks and stems from the tomatillos. Place the tomatillos in water to cover, and gently simmer over low heat until soft, about 30 minutes. Drain. Purée in blender.
4. Combine the tomatillos with the marinated trout, quinoa, tomatoes, onion, red pepper flakes, black peppercorns, and cilantro. Cover and refrigerate for 30 minutes or more. Serve on lettuce leaves.

Variations:
- Substitute sliced avocado for the lettuce.
- Substitute any fresh white fish or shellfish for the trout.
- Substitute fresh lemon juice for lime.
- Substitute chopped serrano chili pepper for red and black pepper.

Pan-Fried Catfish

If you are going fishing, remember to pack a skillet and a pouch of seasoned quinoa flour. That way you can enjoy your catch at its finest—cooked over a fragrant campfire. Prepared indoors with mild-flavored commercial catfish, this dish still retains its natural charm.

Yield: 4 servings
Time: 15 minutes

¼ cup quinoa flour
1 tsp. salt

1. In a large, shallow bowl, combine the quinoa flour, salt, pepper, garlic, and cumin. Rinse the fish under cold water and pat dry. Roll each fillet in the seasoned flour until both sides are covered.
2. Heat a skillet over medium heat and add the

1 tsp. coarsely cracked black pepper
2 tsp. granulated garlic
2 tsp. cumin powder
4 catfish fillets (3 to 4 oz. each)
safflower oil for pan-frying

Garnish:
1 lemon, sliced into wedges

oil. When oil is hot, pan-fry fillets for 3 to 4 minutes on each side, until crisp and browned on the outside and opaque throughout. Serve with lemon wedges.

Variations:
- Substitute perch, flounder, sole, butterfish, shad, bass, turbot, pompano, haddock, red snapper, or trout for the catfish.
- Dot the top with butter or drizzle with safflower oil and broil fillets for 6 to 7 minutes.

Flounder Roll-Ups

The mustard sauce, light, slightly tangy, and sweet, converts a simple dish into an intriguing and sophisticated main course.

Yield: 4 servings
Time: 45 minutes

Pasta:
5 qts. water
1 tsp. salt
½ lb. broad, flat quinoa noodles

Sauce:
1 Tbsp. sesame oil
1 small onion, minced
½ tsp. salt
1 cup vegetable stock
½ cup dry white wine
2 Tbsp. clover honey
2 Tbsp. Dijon mustard
2 sprigs fresh tarragon, minced (or ½ tsp. dried)
1 sprig fresh rosemary, minced (or ¼ tsp. dried)
3 Tbsp. arrowroot flour dissolved in ½ cup cold water

Fish:
4 3 to 4-ounce flounder fillets

1. Bring the water with the salt to a boil. Add pasta. Cook over medium heat until the pasta is tender but still firm to the bite. Drain.
2. Heat a skillet, add the oil, and sauté the onion with the salt over medium heat until limp, about 5 minutes. Add the stock, wine, honey, mustard, tarragon, and rosemary. Bring to a boil over high heat. Stir in the dissolved arrowroot and stir continuously with a whisk until the sauce thickens. Correct the seasoning.
3. Preheat oven to 350°F.
4. Oil an ovenproof serving dish. Set aside 2 tablespoons of the bread crumbs for the topping. Add the remaining bread crumbs to the serving dish and rotate to evenly coat the dish with the crumbs. Place the pasta in the dish and set aside.
5. Rinse the fillets and remove any skin. Slice fillets into strips 1-inch wide. Roll strips into spirals and lay them on top of the pasta. Cover with the mustard sauce. Sprinkle on the remaining bread crumbs. Cover dish loosely with aluminum foil and bake until the fish is opaque throughout, about 10 minutes. Garnish with springs of tarragon.

Variations:
- Substitute other white-fish fillets for the flounder.

Garnish:
- **½ cup bread crumbs**
- **3 sprigs fresh tarragon**

- Substitute milk or soymilk for the vegetable stock.
- Substitute coarse-grained mustard for the Dijon.

Cornish Hens with Quinoa Stuffing

Quinoa's flavor is not immediately apparent in the savory stuffing, but its underlying richness supports the other fine ingredients. The result is an unusual and memorable stuffing.

Prep Tip: The dressing may be made the day before and held in the refrigerator.

Yield: **4 servings**
Time: **1 hour, using cooked quinoa**

Stuffing:
- **1 Tbsp. unsalted butter**
- **2 cloves garlic, minced or pressed**
- **1 small leek, sliced into 1-inch pieces**
- **2 celery ribs with leaves, finely sliced**
- **½ cup fresh porcini mushrooms, sliced fine**
- **½ cup water chestnuts, chopped**
- **3 cups cooked quinoa**
- **5 sprigs fresh sage (or 1 Tbsp. dried)**
- **3 sprig fresh rosemary (or 2 tsp. dried)**
- **3 sprigs fresh thyme (or 2 tsp. dried thyme)**
- **3 Tbsp. dry white wine**
- **1 tsp. tamari or natural soy sauce**
- **½ tsp. freshly ground black pepper**

Hens:
- **2 Cornish hens**
- **½ tsp. salt**
- **2 Tbsp. extra virgin olive oil**
- **2 Tbsp. paprika**

1. Preheat oven to 400°F.
2. Heat a skillet, add butter, and briefly sauté the garlic, leek, celery, porcini, water chestnuts, and quinoa. Stir in the herbs, wine, soy sauce, and pepper, and cook for a few minutes. Adjust seasonings. Set aside.
3. Clean and remove all visible fat from the cavities of the hens. Rub the salt and 1 tablespoon of the olive oil into the birds. Sprinkle surface with 1 tablespoon of the paprika.
4. Loosely stuff each bird. Close with skewers or by securing the legs together. Place remaining stuffing in a small casserole dish and set aside. Arrange stuffed birds in an oiled baking dish and bake in preheated oven for 50 minutes. Mix the remaining olive oil and paprika and use to baste every 15 minutes or so. Bake the extra stuffing during the last 25 minutes that the birds are baking. To serve, slice the hens in half lengthwise. Place each on a plate with the stuffing side down. Garnish with kumquats and cilantro sprigs.

Variations:
- Substitute quinoa corn bread for the quinoa.
- Use this stuffing for fish or other poultry.

Garnish:
2 kumquats, quartered lengthwise
½ bunch cilantro

Chicken, Quinoa, and Spinach

Making the customary chicken and rice dishes like paella, pilaf, stir-fries, and stews becomes an adventure when quinoa is used instead of rice. Classic recipes taste new with quinoa and inspire experimentation with seasonings and additions. Quinoa also has the advantage of cooking in less time than rice.

Yield: 4 servings
Prep Time: 45 minutes, using prepared chicken stock
Total Time: 1 hour

4 chicken breasts
½ tsp. salt
2 Tbsp. safflower oil
1 medium onion, minced
6 to 8 cloves garlic, minced or pressed
1 cup unsalted chicken stock
½ cup dry sherry
3 sprigs fresh lemon thyme, minced (½ tsp. dried)
2 bay leaves
½ cup quinoa
1 lb. fresh spinach
1 tsp. nutmeg
4 oz. Muenster cheese, grated (about 1 cup)

1. Rub the chicken breasts with the salt. Heat a large skillet or casserole over medium heat. Add the oil and brown the chicken for about 4 minutes on each side. Remove chicken and set aside. Sauté the onion and garlic in the same oil for about 3 minutes, until onion is limp.
2. Add the stock, sherry, thyme, and bay leaves. Bring to a boil. Add the quinoa and chicken, reduce heat, and cover. Cook over low heat for 10 minutes.
3. Meanwhile, wash the spinach well and chop leaves into small pieces.
4. Layer the spinach on the quinoa mixture, then sprinkle on the cheese and nutmeg. Replace lid and cook for an additional 10 minutes over low heat.

Variations:
- Substitute quinoa béchamel sauce for the cheese.
- Substitute fresh lima beans for the chicken and vegetable stock for chicken stock.
- Substitute 12 or more ounces of sliced turkey breast for the chicken, substitute kale for the spinach; omit the nutmeg.

Gingered Turkey Egg Rolls

These will resemble the egg rolls that come to your table in Chinese restaurants, but they will have a novel taste. They are filled with a mixture of turkey, quinoa, and vegetables, and flavored with freshly grated ginger.

Yield: 12 rolls
Time: 1 hour, using cooked quinoa and turkey

1 tsp. toasted sesame oil
1 medium onion, minced
3 ribs celery, minced
3 cloves garlic, minced or pressed
¼ tsp. salt
1 Tbsp. ginger juice
1 cup cooked quinoa
1 cup minced turkey
2 Tbsp. natural soy sauce or tamari
12 egg roll skins
peanut oil for shallow pan-frying
hot Chinese mustard for dipping

1. Heat a large skillet or wok. Add the oil and sauté the onion, celery, garlic, and salt. Cover and continue to cook for 10 minutes.
2. Stir ginger juice, quinoa, turkey, and soy sauce into vegetables.
3. Divide the mixture evenly among the egg roll skins. Roll the skins into packets and fry in oil until crisp on all sides. Drain on paper towels or a rack. Serve with mustard.

Variations:
- Serve the filling as a sauce on rice or pasta.
- Omit turkey and use the filling as a stuffing for turkey or other poultry.

Lamb, Quinoa, and Anchovy Ragout

This satisfying and earthy dish is the creation of Felipe Rojas Lombardi, a native of Peru. Long before quinoa was commercially available, Chef Lombardi featured it at his Ballroom Restaurant in New York City. In the following recipe, anchovies, spices and chilies smoothly blend to impart a hearty flavor and a rich brown color to the sauce. Serve the ragout with a crisp green salad.

Prep Tip: The quinoa may be cooked the day before. You may prepare the chili-beer purée and marinate the lamb several hours in advance.

Serves 6 to 8
Time: 90 minutes

2 dried ancho chilies
1 cup dark beer
1 jalapeño chili, blistered, steamed, peeled, and seeded
2 cloves garlic
½ tsp. salt
1 tsp. cumin seeds
8 to 10 anchovies (or 2-oz. can anchovy fillets, drained)
⅛ tsp. ground cloves
⅓ cup balsamic vinegar

1. Soak the ancho chilies in beer until soft, about 20 minutes. Place in blender with jalapeño and blend until smooth. Set aside.
2. Place the garlic in a large mortar and pound it to a paste. Add the salt, cumin, anchovies, and cloves, and pound until smooth. Add the vinegar and mix. Pour this marinade over the lamb pieces. Mix thoroughly and allow to marinate for 20 minutes.
3. In a heavy pot, preferably earthenware, heat the oil. Brown the lamb on all sides. Add the onion and sauté until translucent. Add the anchovy marinade and the chili/beer mixture and cook until the

$2\frac{1}{2}$ lb. lamb (shoulder or leg), bones, trimmed of all visible fat and cut into 1-inch cubes
3 Tbsp. extra virgin olive oil
1 large onion, diced
4 cups vegetable stock
2 cups quinoa

Garnish:
8 to 10 sprigs fresh mint

liquid is almost absorbed. Add the stock, stir, and bring to a boil. Cover, reduce heat, and simmer for 20 to 25 minutes, or until the lamb is tender.
4. Add the quinoa, stir, and cover pot. Continue to cook, stirring occasionally, for 15 minutes. Correct seasoning with salt to taste. Remove from heat. Garnish.

Variations:
- Prepare lamb without quinoa. Serve on a bed of quinoa.
- Substitute seitan for the lamb.

Rutabaga Beef Pot Pie

Here is a one-dish meal that is great cold-weather fare. Rutabagas add rustic flavor to this hearty pie which is covered by a golden, cheddar biscuit crust. Thanks to the food processor, the crust can be assembled in seconds.

Yield: 6 servings
Prep Time: 45 minutes
Total Time: 1 hour, 15 minutes

Beef, Quinoa and Vegetables:
2 Tbsp. unsalted butter
1 lb. stew beef with all visible fat removed, cut into 1-inch cubes
1 large onion, chopped
3 cloves garlic, minced or pressed
5 sprigs fresh savory (or 1 tsp. dried)
1 medium-sized red bell pepper, chopped
1 medium-sized yellow bell pepper, chopped
5 kale leaves, chopped
1 medium rutabaga, with any tough skin peeled off, diced
$\frac{1}{2}$ cup quinoa
$1\frac{1}{2}$ cups chicken stock
2 Tbsp. natural soy sauce or tamari

1. In a large skillet, melt the butter and brown the beef.
2. Add and briefly sauté in the following order: onion, garlic, savory, peppers, kale, rutabaga, and quinoa. Add the stock and bring to a boil. Season with the soy sauce and pepper. Cover, reduce heat and simmer for 15 minutes. Turn into a 10-inch deep-dish pie plate or shallow casserole of similar size.
3. Preheat oven to 350°F.
4. Place the egg, oil, and milk in a processor and blend. Add corn meal, flour, and cheddar and process just to blend. Spoon batter over prepared filling.
5. Bake the pie for about 30 minutes or until the crust is done.

Variations:
- Substitute lamb, chicken, shrimp or seitan for the beef.
- In 1 cup red wine, marinate the beef with the garlic, savory and tamari for 1 to 8 hours. Drain and sauté beef, garlic and savory. Reduce the stock measurement so that the combined stock and remaining marinade total 1 1/2 cups liquid.

$\frac{1}{8}$ tsp. freshly ground black pepper

Crust:
1 egg
1 Tbsp. corn oil
$\frac{1}{2}$ cup milk
$\frac{1}{4}$ cup yellow corn meal
$\frac{1}{2}$ cup quinoa flour
$\frac{1}{2}$ cup grated cheddar cheese

Venison, Quinoa, and Feta in Phyllo

Sublimely rich and delectable, this phyllo is without par. Sally Kane, former head chef at the Sky Line Guest Ranch in Telluride, Colorado, had ample opportunity to please sophisticated palates with game dishes. She served this inspired creation with a shredded carrot-and-cabbage salad dressed with lemon sauce, and followed it with a fresh fruit dessert.

Prep Tip: Prepare the marinade from 10 to 24 hours in advance.

Yield: 6 to 8 servings
Prep Time: 45 minutes, using cooked quinoa
Total Time: 12 hours

Marinade:
1 cup extra virgin olive oil
juice of 2 lemons
dash of Worcestershire sauce
15 juniper berries, chopped
2 cups finely chopped venison
$\frac{1}{3}$ cup unsalted butter
1 medium onion, diced
3 stocks fennel, finely chopped
3 sprigs fresh thyme, chopped (1 tsp. dried)
1 cup crumbled feta cheese
3 cups cooked quinoa
2 Tbsp. whole caraway seed
14 layers phyllo dough

1. In a container with a tight-fitting lid, mix together the olive oil, lemon juice, Worcestershire, juniper berries and venison. Cover and refrigerate for 10 to 24 hours.
2. Preheat oven to 350°F.
3. In a wok or skillet melt the butter. Pour off and reserve all but 1 tablespoon. Now sauté the onion, fennel, and thyme until limp. Remove vegetables to a mixing bowl. Add the feta cheese and quinoa to the vegetables. Mix and set aside.
4. Drain the marinade from the venison. Strain and reserve the liquid. In the same wok or skillet lightly brown the venison.
5. Add venison and 2 tablespoons whole caraway seed to quinoa mixture and mix. Moisten ingredients with enough marinade to make a pudding-like consistency.
6. Oil a 9 by 13-inch baking pan. Have ready a damp—not wet—dish towel, and a soft pastry brush. Remove phyllo dough from its sealed package, lay it on the counter, and cover it with the damp towel. Remove one sheet of phyllo (keep the others under cover) and center it on the baking

pan. Brush this phyllo sheet with some of the reserved melted butter. Extract another phyllo sheet from under the damp towel, position it on the first sheet, and butter it. Repeat to a depth of 8 layers of phyllo.

7. Spread the quinoa/venison mixture evenly over the phyllo. Add 6 more phyllo sheets and butter the first five. Do not butter the top layer. Tuck the phyllo layers around the sides of the pan as if tucking in a blanket. Seal and refrigerate any remaining phyllo sheets.

8. Bake for 35 to 40 minutes or until the top is nicely browned. Cut into large triangles.

Variations:

- For hors d'oeuvres, layer 5 sheets of phyllo brushed with butter on a cookie sheet at least 18 inches by 14 inches. Spread a thinner layer of quinoa mixture over the surface. Top with 4 phyllo sheets (butter only the first 3). Bake and cut into thin rectangles.
- Substitute lamb, or beef for the venison.
- For a vegetarian version, substitute tofu for the feta, seitan for the venison, and olive oil for the butter.

15. Breads, Rolls, Quick Breads, and Crackers

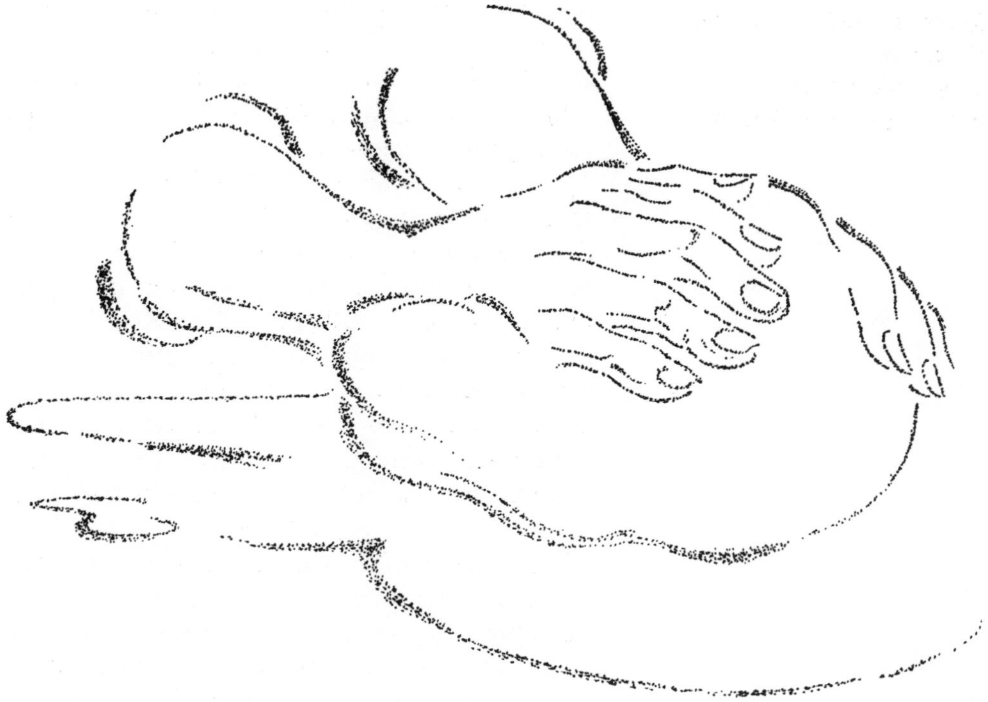

Baguette of Whole Wheat and Quinoa

A new ingredient added to a crusty old loaf yields a richer flavor and a moist, tender crumb. Quinoa flour, like French-grown wheat, is soft, and it enables a closer approximation to an authentic *baguette* than our domestic flour allows. This bread can not be called traditional, but it disappears from the table fast.

Prep Tip: Unlike chemically stabilized white flour, whole grain flours vary from batch to batch. Getting the proper dough consistency (step 3) ensures a successful whole grain loaf.

Yield: 3 loaves, 16 by 3-inches
Prep Time: 30 minutes
Total Time: 4 hours

3 cups warm water
1 Tbsp. active dry yeast
½ cup gluten flour
3 cups unbleached white flour
1½ tsp. salt
2 cups quinoa flour
3 to 5 cups whole wheat flour

1. Pour the warm water into a large bowl. Sprinkle on yeast and allow to soften for 5 minutes.
2. Add the gluten flour and the unbleached flour and beat 100 strokes. Cover and let stand in a warm place for 30 minutes.
3. Stir in the salt and quinoa flour. Add enough wheat flour, a cup at a time, to make a kneadable dough, one that is neither too stiff nor too soft. (Its consistency will be somewhat stickier than that of a dough made from all white flour.) Turn onto a lightly floured board and knead until shiny and elastic, 5 to 10 minutes.
4. Place the dough in an oiled bowl, cover, and set in a warm place for 1 1/2 hours or until almost doubled in bulk. Punch down and knead in the bowl for several strokes. Cover and let rise again until it doubles in bulk, about 1 hour.
5. Divide the dough into 3 equal pieces. Pull and roll into sausage shapes with tapered ends. Place in a lightly oiled, long French-bread pan or on an oiled baking sheet. Cover and let rise in a warm place about 15 minutes, or until doubled in bulk.
6. Preheat oven to 425°F. Pour 2 inches water into a large ovenproof dish and place on the oven floor to create steam. Slash the breads diagonally, making three parallel gashes. Place in oven and bake for 10 minutes. Remove from oven and brush with water. Reduce heat to 375°F. and bake an additional 40 minutes or until the loaves sound hollow when the bottoms are rapped with the knuckles.

Variations:

- Brush tops with garlic butter while they are still hot.

See Glossary for descriptions of unfamiliar ingredients.
See Appendix for information on quinoa flour, chilies and natural sugar.

- For a golden-colored bread, dissolve a scant 1/2 teaspoon ground saffron in 1 tablespoon hot water. Add with the gluten flour.
- After shaping the loaves, roll them in sesame seeds.
- Toast and butter slices; break them into a bowl of warm milk for milk-toast.

Quinoa-Enriched White Bread

Unlike most white breads, this one actually supplies valuable nutrients, thanks to the addition of quinoa. It has a crunchy crust and a chewy inside that remains moist for days.

Yield: 3 loaves
Prep Time: ½ hour
Total Time: 3 ½ hours

3 Tbsp. clover honey
3¾ cups warm milk
1 Tbsp. active dry yeast
3 cups unbleached white flour
1½ cups cooked quinoa
¼ cup sesame oil
2 tsp. salt
5 to 7 cups unbleached white flour

1. Add honey to warm milk and stir to dissolve. Sprinkle on yeast and allow to stand 5 minutes.
2. Add the 3 cups of flour and beat 100 strokes. Cover and let stand in a warm place for 40 minutes or until doubled in bulk.
3. Add the quinoa, oil, salt, and enough of the additional flour to make a kneadable dough. Turn onto floured surface and knead until shiny and elastic, 5 to 10 minutes.
4. Place the dough in an oiled bowl, cover, and set in a warm place for 40 minutes or until the dough doubles in bulk. Punch down, cover, and let rise another 40 minutes, or until the volume doubles.
5. Preheat oven to 350°F. Divide the dough into three equal pieces. Shape each into a smooth loaf. Set in oiled bread pans. Cover and let rise 10 minutes.
6. Place in a hot oven and bake for 45 to 50 minutes, or until the bottom of the loaf sounds hollow when rapped with the knuckles.

Variations:

- For cinnamon rolls, cover the bottom of an 8-inch-square pan with 1 tablespoon melted, unsalted butter. Roll out 1/3 of the twice-risen dough into a rectangle. Sprinke with pecans, plumped raisins, natural sugar, and cinnamon. Roll tightly into a sausage shape. Cut into pieces 3 inches wide and set in the oiled pan. Bake at 400°F for 25 minutes or until browned.

- Brush the surface with egg white after baking.
- Use different flours: substitute up to 1 cup barley, millet, oat, rye, buckwheat, or corn flour for the white flour.

Whole Wheat Sourdough

The beauty of this sourdough is that it needs no starter because the entire loaf acts as the starter. It rises as the grains ferment naturally. Not many breads have as much whole grain goodness—whole in the sense of being unrefined and also in the sense of being unbroken, since cooked quinoa is used. Breads do not get much simpler—or more appealing—than this. The bread will keep up to 2 weeks refrigerated.

Prep Tips: If the cooked quinoa has been at room temperature for a day, the leavening process will be hastened. If the dough shows no visible signs of rising after 24 hours, move it to a warmer location, still covered, and bake when it has risen to the top of the dish. A glass bread pan is recommended for proofing and baking because the crust would taste metallic after sitting in a metal pan for a whole day. (If your baking dish is clear glass, you can watch the dough becoming aerated and spongy during proofing.) The bread can cool in the pan before removing. For thin slices, cool thoroughly before slicing.

Yield: 1 loaf
Prep Time: 15 minutes, using cooked quinoa
Total Time: 24–36 hours

3½ cups whole wheat flour
½ tsp. salt
1 cup cooked, cooled quinoa
1¼ cups spring water*
2 Tbsp. sesame oil

1. Combine 3 cups of the flour with the salt in a large mixing bowl. Add the quinoa, water, and oil. Using a wooden paddle or spoon, mix all of the ingredients until the liquid has been thoroughly incorporated.
2. Set the dough on a lightly floured surface and knead for 5 minutes, adding additional flour as necessary to prevent sticking.
3. Shape into a loaf; turn into an oiled glass bread pan. Press firmly into the pan. Lightly oil the surface. Cover the dish snugly with plastic wrap.
4. Set the loaf in a warm place for about 24 hours. When it has risen to the top of the dish, remove the plastic, being careful not to tear surface of the dough. Do not punch down.
5. Place in a cold oven. Set temperature at 325°F and bake for 1 hour or until edges pull away from the sides.

* The chlorine in municipal tap water inhibits fermentation. If tap water is used, boil it first for 5 minutes to eliminate the chlorine.

Grissini (Bread Sticks) with Quinoa Nuggets

Soft quinoa flour and quality olive oil impart a tender and moist inner crumb to Italian bread sticks. The quinoa crunches decorate and flavor the whole length of the crusty *grissini.* Serve them warm, or allow them to cool thoroughly and stand upright in a tall, narrow basket. Home gardeners who have a black variety of quinoa should not miss this opportunity to show off their colors.

Prep Tip: For the precise grissini texture, mix and shape the dough as gently as you would a pie crust.

Yield: 30 10-inch bread sticks
Prep Time: 30 minutes
Total Time: 1 ½ hours

⅓ cup water
½ cup quinoa
1 Tbsp. active dry yeast
1 cup warm water
2 Tbsp. extra virgin olive oil
1½ cups unbleached white flour
1½ cups quinoa flour
2 Tbsp. natural sugar
½ tsp. salt
¼ cup arrowroot flour
¼ cup water

1. Bring the 1/3 cup water to a boil. Add the quinoa, cover, remove from the heat, and set aside.
2. Sprinkle the yeast on the 1 cup of warm water and allow it to soften for 5 minutes.
3. Sift together the flours, salt, and sugar. Rub the oil into the flour mixture with your finger tips. Mix the yeast mixture and the parched quinoa into the dry ingredients just until a ball is formed. Use a light touch and do not overmix. Cover and allow to rest for 20 minutes.
4. With a light hand, pinch off approximately 2 tablespoons of dough. Shape it into a 10-inch long stick, a finger-width in diameter, and place it upon an oiled cookie sheet. Repeat until all the dough is shaped. Cover and allow to rest for 30 minutes.
5. Preheat oven to 375°F.
6. Brush sticks with arrowroot dissolved in water. Bake in a hot oven for 12 minutes or just until browned.

Variations:

- To make chapati, pinch off a walnut-sized piece of proofed dough. Roll out to a 7-inch diameter and cook both sides on a seasoned skillet.

Pumpernickel Rolls

I like to shape this dough into rolls rather than make it into bread, but that is not to say that this same recipe does not make a tasty sandwich loaf. The grain coffee powder imparts a warm brown color and the quinoa gives it satisfying texture.

Yield: 12 rolls
Prep Time: 30 minutes
Total Time: 2 ½ hours

2 Tbsp. clover honey
2 cups warm water
2 tsp. active dry yeast
2 cups gluten flour
1 cup cooked, cooled quinoa
2 Tbsp. grain coffee powder
1 Tbsp. sesame oil
1 tsp. salt
3 to 4 cups rye flour

Glaze:
1 egg
¼ cup dill seed

1. Add the honey to the warm water and stir to dissolve. Sprinkle on yeast and allow to stand 5 minutes.
2. Add the gluten flour and beat 100 strokes. Cover, and let stand in a warm place 40 minutes or until doubled in bulk.
3. Add the quinoa, grain coffee powder, oil, salt, and enough of the rye flour to make a kneadable dough. Turn onto a surface floured with the rye flour and knead until shiny and elastic, about 5 minutes.
4. Place the dough in an oiled bowl, cover, and set in a warm place 40 minutes, or until doubled in bulk. Punch down, cover, and let rise another 40 minutes, or until the volume doubles.
5. Preheat oven to 350°F. Divide the dough into 12 equal pieces. Knead each into a smooth ball. Set on an oiled baking sheet, cover, and let stand 5 minutes.
6. Crack the egg into a small bowl and lightly beat with a whisk. Place the dill seed in another small bowl. Dip top of each roll into egg, then into dill seeds. Place the rolls on an oiled baking sheet and bake 25 minutes or until nicely browned.

Variations:
- Substitute caraway or fennel seeds, minced onion, or a combination of these for the dill seed.
- Shape dough into 16 bagels instead of 12 rolls, boil in water for 5 minutes before baking. Add poppy seeds just before baking.
- Bake in muffin tins.
- Substitute unbleached white flour for the gluten flour.

Quinoa Corn Pone

This classic combination of corn and quinoa could not be more simple or delicious. Corn pone sticks, a specialty of Alabama, are typically made in pone pans with corn-shaped wells. The pone's crumbly outside makes a great texture contrast to its almost puddinglike inside.

Yield: 18 corn sticks
Prep Time: 10 minutes
Total Time: 25 minutes

2 cups water
¼ tsp. salt
2 Tbsp. unsalted butter
1 cup quinoa flour
1 cup white corn meal

1. Preheat oven to 425°F. Oil the corn pone pan and put it in oven to heat.
2. In a small pot bring the water and salt to a boil. Add and melt the butter. Remove from heat.
3. With a few rapid strokes, blend water mixture with flour and corn meal. It will be a stiff batter. Spoon the batter into the wells of the hot pone pan. Bake for 12 minutes or until browned.

Variations:
- Make corn sticks on a cookie sheet by spooning batter, then shaping it into oblongs.
- Bake as muffins or corn bread.

Picante Quinoa Corn Bread

This light, zippy corn bread goes great with a south-of-the-border meal. It retains its moisture longer than a bread that is made only with corn.

Prep Tip: For maximum flavor, allow the batter to rest for 30 minutes before baking.

Yield: 8 by 8-inch square corn bread
Prep Time: 10 minutes
Total Time: 1 hour

1 cup quinoa flour
1 cup yellow corn meal
4 tsp. baking powder
5 sprigs fresh marjoram (1 Tbsp. dried marjoram)
2 tsp. orange zest
1 Tbsp. red chili powder
¼ tsp. salt
¼ cup unsalted butter
2 eggs, beaten
1 cup milk
1 Anaheim chili, blistered, steamed, peeled and diced
1 poblano chili, blistered, steamed, peeled and diced

1. Preheat oven to 375°F.
2. Mix together the flour, corn meal, baking powder, marjoram, orange zest, chili powder, and salt. Set aside.
3. Melt the butter in a small skillet. In a mixing bowl, lightly beat the eggs and stir in the milk and melted butter. With a few quick strokes, blend the wet and dry ingredients and the chilies.
4. Spoon into oiled, 8 by 8-inch pan. Bake for 20 minutes or until the corn bread starts to brown and a toothpick inserted in the center comes out clean.

Variations:
- Add 1/2 cup grated sharp cheese.
- For a dairy-free bread, substitute soymilk, corn oil and 4 ounces of tofu in place of the milk, butter and egg.
- Make one dozen muffins instead of a pan bread.

Blue Corn and Quinoa Bread

This substantial, unleavened bread is not made for a delicate presentation or to serve alongside a heavy meal. It is almost a meal in itself and is one of my favorite, energy-supplying backpacking foods. It remains fresh for several days and is scrumptious when pan-fried. Vital foods such as blue corn and quinoa stand well by themselves without the addition of other flavorings. Foods cooked in earthenware are subtly enhanced, so for best results bake this in an earthenware casserole.

Prep Tip: To improve the flavor and increase digestibility, parch the corn by pouring boiling water over it and allowing it to rest prior to mixing with quinoa.

Yield: 1 round, 9-inches in diameter
Prep Time: 10 minutes
Total Time: 3 ½ hours

2½ cups water
1 tsp. salt
5 cups blue corn meal
2½ cups cooked quinoa
½ cup quinoa or wheat flour
2 tsp. chia seeds

1. Bring the water and salt to a boil. Place the blue corn meal in a mixing bowl, add the boiling water, and stir to blend. Cover with a tea towel and allow to rest from 2 to 8 hours.
2. Oil a 9-inch earthenware casserole. Using your hands, mix in the cooked quinoa and the flour to form a sticky and thick dough. Turn into the prepared casserole. With moistened hand, spread and smooth batter into the casserole. Sprinkle with the chia seeds. Cover and place in a cold oven. Turn to 350°F. and bake for 1 hour and 20 minutes. Uncover and bake an additional 10 minutes or until the bread is browned on top and is pulling away from the edges of the casserole.

Variations:

- Slice the bread and pan-fry in butter. Season with soy sauce for a savory dish or top with maple syrup or jam.
- Mix in diced onion and diced chili with the quinoa.
- Substitute quinoa cooked with millet or with corn (page 69 or 70) for quinoa.

Garbanzo-Quinoa Muffins

Garbanzo flour, a standard ingredient of Middle Eastern and East Indian cookery, is now available in specialty food markets. It imparts a rich, chickenlike flavor to dumplings and quick breads. When it is combined with a grain, as below, the result is a complete protein. This muffin is substantial but not heavy. Dude-ranch chef, Sally Kane, from Colorado's San Juan mountain range, created it to go with partridge and other poultry dishes.

Prep Tip: Garbanzo flour is slow to brown so these muffins need close watching to prevent overcooking.

Yield: 18 muffins
Prep Time: 10 minutes, using cooked quinoa
Total Time: 40 minutes

1 egg
¼ cup unsalted butter
1¼ cups milk
1½ cups cooked, cooled quinoa
¼ cup chopped parsley
1½ cups unbleached white flour
1½ cups garbanzo flour
1 tsp. ground cumin
1¼ tsp. ground coriander
⅓ tsp. chili powder
1 tsp. baking soda
1 tsp. baking powder
½ tsp. salt

1. Preheat oven to 350°F.
2. Mix together the eggs, oil, and milk. Stir in the quinoa and parsley.
3. Sift together flours, spices, baking soda and powder, and salt. Stir wet mixture into dry ingredients just enough to combine ingredients. Spoon into an oiled muffin tin and bake for 30 minutes or until they just start to brown.

Variation:

- Substitute soymilk for milk, increase baking soda to 2 teaspoons, eliminate baking powder, and add 1 tablespoon fresh lemon juice.

Blue Corn Cranberry Muffins

Quickly made muffins are the busy cook's lifesaver. Ruby cranberries, lavender corn, and pearly quinoa combine to create this outstanding muffin of inimitable flavor and crumb. I enjoy serving these gems fresh out of the oven for breakfast or afternoon tea.

Prep Tip: Frozen cranberries may be added directly to the batter if they are free from icy condensation.

Yield: 18 muffins
Prep Time: 10 minutes
Total Time: 30 minutes

1½ cups quinoa flour
1½ cups blue corn meal
1 tsp. baking powder
1 tsp. baking soda
½ tsp. salt
¼ cup unsalted butter
2 eggs
½ cup maple syrup
¾ cup milk
1 cup fresh cranberries

1. Preheat oven to 375°F.
2. Sift together quinoa flour, corn meal, baking powder, baking soda, and salt.
3. Melt butter and allow to cool. Beat the eggs. Add maple syrup, butter, and milk. Gently stir into the dry ingredients, being careful not to overmix. Mix in the cranberries.
4. Spoon into oiled muffin tins. Bake for 20 minutes or until muffins start to brown and a toothpick inserted into the center comes out clean.

Variations:

- Substitute 1 cup blueberries for the cranberries.

- Substitute yellow or white corn meal for the blue corn meal.
- Add 1 cup chopped macadamia nuts.

Golden Muffins

Start these muffins the night before and look forward to eating them for breakfast. They are colorful, crunchy, and taste like the marmalade's already on them because of the sweet and winey sultanas and the orange rind. Use organic oranges, or scrub the rind well before grating.

Yield: 12 muffins
Prep Time: 10 minutes
Total Time: 40 minutes

1¼ cups boiling water
1 cup quinoa
1 cup yellow corn meal
½ cup sultana raisins
¼ cup clover honey
¼ cup corn oil
1 egg, beaten
zest from 1 orange
½ tsp. salt
1¼ cups whole wheat pastry flour
2 tsps. baking powder

1. Pour the boiling water over the quinoa, corn meal, and raisins. Stir to moisten, cover and let stand for 1 to 8 hours.
2. Preheat oven to 375°F. Oil muffin tins. Stir into the quinoa mixture the honey, oil, egg, orange zest, salt, flour, and baking powder. Mix quickly, being careful not to overmix. Spoon into oiled muffin tins. Bake for 30 minutes or until lightly browned.

Variation:

- Substitute fresh currants for the sultanas.

Currant Scones

More like cake than bread, these are similar to a traditional scone made of barley or oat flour. Scones take so little effort to make and are great for breakfast, lunch or supper. For a definitive Devonshire tea, serve scones—hot or cold—with clotted cream and jam. For a southern-style breakfast call them biscuits and serve them with gravy.

Yield: 12 scones
Prep Time: 15 minutes
Total Time: 30 minutes

1 cup quinoa flour
1 cup unbleached white flour

1. Preheat oven to 425°F.
2. Sift together the flours, sugar, salt, baking powder, and baking soda.
3. Cut the butter into small pieces. Cut butter pieces into the dry ingredients until the mixture resembles coarse meal with some pea-sized pieces remaining.

$\frac{1}{3}$ cup natural sugar
$\frac{1}{2}$ tsp. salt
$1\frac{1}{2}$ tsp. baking powder
$\frac{1}{2}$ tsp. baking soda
$\frac{1}{2}$ cup unsalted butter
2 tsp. orange zest
$\frac{1}{3}$ cup currants
$\frac{1}{2}$ cup buttermilk plus some for brushing on scone tops

4. Add the zest and currants. Toss gently to coat. Gradually add butter milk until dough just holds together.
5. Turn the dough onto a lightly floured board and roll it to 3/4-inch thickness. Using a 2-inch-round cookie cutter, cut out circles of dough. Place on an oiled baking sheet. Brush tops with buttermilk. Bake for 12 to 15 minutes or until golden.

Variation:
- For strawberry shortcake, roll dough to 1-inch thickness. Bake. Slice fresh strawberries, sweeten, and season with basalmic vinegar. Sandwich prepared strawberries between biscuits. Add a dollop of whipped cream.

Seedy Quinoa Crackers

You will not be able to eat just one of these crackers. Thin, crisp, and speckled, they are decidedly more interesting and tasty than any kind bought in a store. And they take such little time and effort to prepare.

Prep Tips: For the most delicious taste, roll the dough out thin. The dough may be made a day in advance. Quinoa crackers, once cooled, keep for a week or more in an airtight jar.

Yield: 48 crackers
Prep Time: 10 minutes
Total Time: 25 minutes

Cracker:
1 cup quinoa flour
1 cup unbleached white flour
1 tsp. black sesame seeds
2 tsp. hulled sesame seeds
1 tsp. baking powder
$\frac{1}{2}$ tsp. salt
1 tsp. roasted sesame oil
3 Tbsp. sesame oil
$\frac{1}{2}$ to $\frac{2}{3}$ cup water

Glaze:
2 tsp. natural soy sauce or tamari
2 tsp. sesame oil

1. Combine flours, seeds, baking powder, and salt in a medium-sized mixing bowl. With finger tips, rub in the oils. Add water in three stages to form a workable but soft dough. Cover and let rest 10 minutes.
2. Preheat oven to 425°F. Roll out the cracker dough on a large, oiled, open-sided baking sheet to 1/16-inch thickness. Cut into 1 1/2-inch strips. Cut strips on the diagonal to create diamond-shaped crackers.
3. In a small saucer combine the soy sauce and oil. Brush glaze over the crackers. Bake for 5 to 7 minutes or until the crackers are lightly browned. Cool on rack.

Variations:
- Substitute butter for the oils.
- Roll dough out on a floured board and cut with cookie cutters.

Assorted quinoa cookies

Quinoa Rye bagels (see Pumpernickel Roll Variation, page 149–59)

16. Desserts

Cranberry Lime Cake

This cake is colorful, refreshing, and easy to make, The perky lime blends with quinoa's slight tang to enliven an old standby. It is a delectable cake that everyone loves.

Prep Tip: The batter looks dry, but it bakes fine. Because the cake rests overnight in the pan, bake it in a ceramic bundt mold or a glass cake pan. For best results use *fine* quinoa flour and natural sugar. If the sugar is lumpy, first pulverize it in a blender.

Yield: 1 10-inch bundt cake
Prep Time: 25 minutes
Total Time: 10 hours

1½ cups quinoa flour
1½ cups unbleached white flour
1 tsp. baking soda
1 tsp. baking powder
½ tsp. salt
1½ cups whole cranberries
1½ cups chopped dates
1 cup chopped pecans
3½ tsp. grated lime peel (about 4 limes)
¼ cup unsalted butter
1 cup natural sugar
2 eggs, lightly beaten
1 cup buttermilk

Glaze:
1 cup natural sugar
¾ cup fresh lime juice (about 4 limes)

1. Preheat oven to 350°F.
2. Sift together the flours, baking soda, baking powder, and salt. Stir in the cranberries, dates, pecans, and lime peel.
3. Cream the butter and sugar. Stir in the eggs and buttermilk. Add to dry ingredients and mix just until blended. Pour into an oiled pan. Bake until a toothpick inserted in the center comes out clean, about 50 minutes. Cool on a rack for 15 minutes, but do not remove the cake from the pan.
4. To prepare the glaze, cook the sugar and lime juice in a small, heavy saucepan over low heat, stirring occasionally, until the sugar dissolves. Pour over the warm cake. Let stand in the pan at room temperature overnight. To serve, invert cake onto a platter.

Variations:
- Replace the white flour with corn flour, eliminate step 4, bake in muffin tins, and serve as a rich breakfast muffin.
- Substitute whole wheat flour for the unbleached white flour and soymilk for the buttermilk.
- Omit the dates and pecans.

Double Rich Chocolate Quinoa Cake

Quinoa flour transforms an everyday chocolate cake into a tantalizing and distinctive dessert, one that makes an unforgettable ending to a meal. This cake will stay fresh for days—if you can keep it around that long.

Prep Tip: For a light texture, use extra fine quinoa flour. If natural sugar is lumpy, blend it in a blender to a fine powder. The cake may be prepared (but not iced) one day in advance. Cool thoroughly and wrap in plastic.

See Glossary for descriptions of unfamiliar ingredients.
See Appendix for information on quinoa flour, chilies and natural sugar.

Yield: 1 9-inch, double-layer cake
Prep Time: 25 minutes
Total Time: 1 ½ hours

Cake:
- 3 oz. unsweetened chocolate
- 1 cup fine quinoa flour
- 1⅓ cups unbleached white flour
- 1 tsp. baking powder
- ¾ tsp. baking soda
- ½ tsp. salt
- ¾ cup unsalted butter, softened
- 2 cups natural sugar
- 1½ cups milk
- 3 eggs, lightly beaten
- 1 tsp. vanilla

Icing:
- 3 oz. cream cheese
- 1½ Tbsp. milk
- ¾ cup natural sugar
- 1½ tsp. lemon zest

Filling and Decoration:
- ⅓ cup apricot jam
- ¾ cup toasted almond slices

1. Preheat oven to 350°F.
2. Melt the chocolate in a double boiler. Set aside.
3. Sift together the flours, baking powder, baking soda, and salt.
4. Cream the butter and sugar. Add the milk, eggs, vanilla, and melted chocolate. Mix wet ingredients with dry ingredients. Pour into two oiled and floured 9-inch layer pans. Bake for 40 minutes or until a toothpick inserted into centers comes out clean. Cool in pans 10 minutes. Remove from pans and finish cooling on racks.
5. To make the icing, cream together the cheese and milk until soft and fluffy. Gradually beat in the sugar and add lemon zest.
6. Place one cooled cake flat-side up on a platter. Spread with jam. Position the second cake on top. Cover the entire cake with frosting. Press almond slices into sides of cake.

Variations:
- Substitute stiff whipped cream for the cream cheese icing.
- Substitute 1/4 cup strong, cold coffee for the 1/4 cup milk.
- Add 1/4 teaspoon mint extract to batter.
- Substitute chocolate shavings for the almond slices.

Peachy Quinoa Spice Cake

As a child, my favorite cake was my mother's Poor Man's Cake. Here is mom's recipe which is upgraded with quinoa, but lacks her homemade maraschino cherries. For those with wheat allergies, this fruity, old-fashioned cake is wheat free.

Yield: 1 9-inch tube cake
Prep Time: 10 minutes
Total Time: 50 minutes

- 1¾ cups quinoa flour
- ½ cup chopped dates
- 1 cup currants
- ½ cup chopped pecans
- ½ tsp. baking soda
- ½ tsp. baking powder
- ½ tsp. salt

1. Preheat oven to 350°F.
2. Sprinkle 1/4 cup of the quinoa flour over the dates, currants, and pecans, and set fruits aside. Blend the baking soda, baking powder, salt, cinnamon and cloves with the remaining quinoa flour.
3. Cream together the butter and sugar.
4. Remove pits from the peaches, but leave the skins intact. Place in a processor or blender and blend until smooth. Beat in the egg. Combine with creamed butter and sugar. Add the fruit and nuts

1 tsp. cinnamon
½ tsp. ground cloves
½ cup unsalted butter
1 cup natural sugar
2 medium-sized fully ripened peaches
1 egg

to dry ingredients. Add wet ingredients to dry and mix well.

5. Spoon into an oiled 9-inch tube pan and bake for 40 to 45 minutes or until a toothpick inserted in the center comes out clean. Serve as is, or top each serving with Maple Syrup Glaze (recipe follows).

Variations:

- Substitute grated carrot for the peaches. Replace the ground cloves with cardamom powder and replace raisins for the dates and currants.
- Use 1 cup thick, unsweetened applesauce instead of peaches.
- Add 1 teaspoon ground ginger to make a gingerbread.
- Substitute 2 bananas for the peach sauce. Replace the cinnamon and cloves with 1/2 teaspoon anise extract.

Maple Syrup Glaze

This glaze easily substitutes as a hot syrup for waffles and pancakes. It lends itself to endless embellishments, and thanks to the *kuzu*, is soothing to the digestive tract.

Prep Tips: To facilitate the measuring of *kuzu*, pulverize lumps with the back of a spoon and then measure it. When reheating a cooled *kuzu* preparation, thin with additional liquid.

Yield: 1 cup
Time: 5 minutes

2½ tsp. kuzu
¾ cup peach nectar or apple juice
¼ cup maple syrup
⅛ tsp. nutmeg

Garnish:
¼ cup ground pecans

1. Dissolve the kuzu in 2 tablespoons juice.
2. In a small saucepan, bring maple syrup and remaining juice to a boil.
3. Stir in dissolved kuzu, return to a boil, and simmer, stirring constantly, for 1 minute, or until thick, translucent and smooth. Remove from heat. Stir in nutmeg.
4. Spoon over individual cake servings. Top with a sprinkle of pecans.

Variations:

- Substitute cinnamon for the nutmeg.
- Substitute arrowroot flour for the kuzu.
- Add a drop of almond extract and replace the pecans with almonds.
- Add 1/2 teaspoon orange zest and substitute orange juice for the peach nectar.

Pineapple Coconut Cake

This dairy-and-wheat-free cake gets its golden color from both quinoa flour and pineapple. Moist, creamy, and tangy-sweet, its aroma fills the whole house as it bakes.

Yield: 1 9½-inch bundt cake, 3 inches high
Prep Time: 15 minutes
Time: 1½ hours

2 eggs, separated
1 cup diced unsweetened pineapple
~~**¾ cup unsweetened pineapple juice**~~ -CAN JUICE ONLY.
¼ cup safflower oil
½ cup orange blossom honey
1 tsp. vanilla
2 cups quinoa flour
1 cup unsweetened coconut
1 tsp. baking soda
½ tsp. ground cardamom
¼ tsp. salt

Topping:
2 Tbsp. orange blossom honey
2 Tbsp. unsweetened coconut

1. Preheat oven to 350°F.
2. In a food processor, place the egg yolks, pineapple, pineapple juice, oil, honey, and vanilla. Process until thoroughly mixed.
3. Whip the egg whites until stiff but not dry.
4. In a mixing bowl, combine the quinoa flour, coconut, baking soda, cardamom, and salt. Add wet ingredients to dry. Stir well. Fold in the whipped egg whites. Pour into an oiled bundt cake pan. Bake for 1 hour. Cool. Invert onto a plate.
5. Heat the honey. Drizzle it over the cake, then sprinkle with coconut.

Variations:
- Add up to 1/2 cup chopped pecans or macadamia nuts to the batter.
- Substitute 1 1/2 cups mashed banana for the pineapple and juice.

Steamed Date Cake

Steamed cakes are naturally moist and tend to stay that way. For holiday giving, friends who have wheat allergies will appreciate this fruitcake. It travels well in the mail. After it has cooled, slice it thin to show off the generous cross-sections of dates and walnuts.

Prep Tip: Glass bakeware is recommended because it leaves no metallic taste if the cake cools in the pan. If you steam the cake in a metal utensil, remove it to cool.

Yield: 1 8 by 4 by 2-inch loaf
Prep Time: 15 minutes
Total Time: 1 hour, 15 minutes

1 cup walnuts
3 cups Deglit Noor dates, pitted and chopped

1. Heat oven to 250°F. Place the walnuts on a baking sheet and roast in oven for 10 minutes.
2. Combine the walnuts, dates, apple juice concentrate, orange juice and zest, nutmeg, and salt. Add the quinoa flour. Work mixture with hands to blend all ingredients.
3. Press into an oiled, glass loaf pan. Cover tightly with aluminum foil. Set on a steaming rack

$\frac{1}{3}$ cup frozen apple juice concentrate
juice and zest from 1 orange
$\frac{1}{2}$ tsp. nutmeg
$\frac{1}{4}$ tsp. salt
$1\frac{1}{4}$ cups quinoa flour

in a pot with 2 to 3 inches of water. Cover and steam for 1 hour over boiling water, replenishing water as necessary. Cool thoroughly before slicing.

Variations:
- Substitute figs for the dates.
- Substitute diced pineapple for part of the dates and substitute frozen orange-pineapple juice concentrate for the apple juice.

Sour Cream Fudge Cupcakes

I find cupcakes to be irresistible, especially rich chocolate ones. The quinoa flour gives these a tender and moist crumb—as it does to all baked goods. They are moist enough to stand alone, but no one will complain if you dress them up with an icing.

Yield: 12 cupcakes
Prep Time: 15 minutes
Total Time: 35 minutes

$\frac{1}{4}$ cup unsalted butter
$\frac{1}{2}$ cup water
$\frac{1}{4}$ cup cocoa powder
1 cup natural sugar
$1\frac{1}{4}$ cups quinoa flour
$\frac{1}{2}$ tsp. baking powder
$\frac{1}{2}$ tsp. baking soda
$\frac{1}{2}$ tsp. salt
2 eggs, separated
$\frac{1}{2}$ tsp. vanilla
$\frac{1}{4}$ cup sour cream

1. Preheat oven to 375°F.
2. Add the butter to the water in a saucepan. Bring to a boil, remove from heat, and whisk in the cocoa powder.
3. Sift together the natural sugar, quinoa flour, baking powder, baking soda, and salt. Add the cooled cocoa mixture, egg yolks, vanilla, and sour cream, and blend well.
4. Beat the egg whites until stiff but not dry. Fold into batter.
5. Spoon into a muffin tin lined with paper cupcake-liners. Bake for 20 minutes, or until a cake tester inserted in center comes out clean.

Variations:
- Add 1/2 cup chopped walnuts or pecans to the batter, or sprinkle a few chopped nuts on top of each cupcake.
- Add 1/4 teaspoon mint extract to the batter.
- Substitute peanut butter for the butter.
- Bake as a cake in an 8 by 8-inch pan for 30 to 35 minutes.
- Substitute yogurt for the sour cream.

Plum Tart

An open tart, with overlapping plums, this extraordinary pastry looks elaborate but is surprisingly quick and easy to make. Guests and family will long remember its appearance and taste.

Yield: 1 9-inch tart
Prep Time: 20 minutes
Total Time: 2 hours

Crust:
- **½ cup quinoa flour**
- **½ cup unbleached white flour**
- **few grains of salt**
- **1 Tbsp. natural sugar, sifted**
- **¼ tsp. orange zest**
- **3 Tbsp. unsalted butter, at room temperature**
- **2 Tbsp. water**
- **½ tsp. vanilla**

Filling:
- **2 cups washed and halved pitted plums**
- **⅓ cup natural sugar**
- **¼ cup butter**

Garnish:
- **½ cup heavy cream, whipped with 1 Tbsp. Kirsch**

1. Place the flours, salt, sugar, and orange zest in a bowl and cut in the butter to form a coarse meal.
2. Combine the water and vanilla, and stir into the flour mixture. Mix lightly, just enough to form the pastry into a ball, adding up to 1 additional tablespoon water if necessary. Cover with waxed paper or plastic. Allow to rest, refrigerated or in a cool place, for 30 minutes.
3. Preheat oven to 400°F. Roll the dough out between two sheets of waxed paper. Place dough in a springform pan.
4. Starting from the edge, arrange the plum halves in the tart shell. Overlap plums to create a spiral design. Sprinkle with the sugar. Cut butter into thin pats and dot on plums. Place tart in a hot oven and bake for 45 to 50 minutes or until the crust is golden. Allow to cool 10 minutes. Remove sides from pan.
5. Cut tart into wedges. Garnish with a dollop of whipped cream.

Variations:
- Use pears, nectarines, or peaches instead of the plums.
- Double the crust recipe and cover the plums with a top crust.

Lemon Pie in Chocolate Quinoa Crust

It is hard to say which is more delicious—the fudgey bottom of this pie or its delicate, "citrusy" filling of tiny tapiocalike quinoa.

Prep Tip: For best results, allow to cool naturally, then serve. If refrigerated, the filling settles and loses its light quality.

Yield: 1 9-inch pie
Prep Time: 30 minutes, using cooked quinoa
Total Time: 1 hour, 15 minutes

Crust:
- **1 cup quinoa flour**
- **2 Tbsp. cocoa powder**
- **¼ tsp. salt**
- **½ cup unsalted butter**
- **2 Tbsp. orange blossom honey**
- **1 tsp. minced orange zest**

Filling:
- **2 eggs, separated**
- **juice and zest of 1 medium lemon**
- **1 cup cooked, cooled quinoa**
- **½ cup orange blossom honey**
- **⅛ tsp. salt**

1. Combine the quinoa flour, cocoa powder, and salt. Using a pastry cutter, two forks, or a food processor, cut the butter into the flour mixture. Add the honey and zest. Butter the bottom and sides of a 9-inch springform pan. Spread the dough evenly across the bottom of the pan.
2. Preheat oven to 325°F.
3. Beat the egg whites until stiff but not dry.
4. With a whisk, combine the egg yolks, lemon juice and zest, quinoa, honey, and salt. Gently fold in the beaten egg whites.
5. Pour the mixture into the crust. Bake for 40 to 45 minutes or until a knife inserted in the center comes out clean. Allow to cool. Gently run knife around edge of pie and remove sides of pan.

Variations:
- Substitute orange or a combination of lemon and lime for lemon in filling.
- Substitute pecan pie filling or any chiffon pie filling for lemon-quinoa filling.
- Prebake crust for 20 to 25 minutes. Cool, fill with softened ice cream or frozen yogurt and freeze until serving.
- Add ground almonds to crust.

Maple Walnut Pie in Quinoa Crust

To call it "rich" does not do justice to this maple-walnut pie. The pastry is golden and delicate, the filling is sweet and buttery. It is perfect for holiday celebrations as it can be prepared ahead of time and served to 10 or 12 people. Top it with whipped cream or a scoop of vanilla ice cream. It can be refrigerated for up to 4 days.

Prep Tip: By using a food processor, the filling can be prepared in less than a minute. Simply process all filling ingredients except nuts until smooth. Add the nuts and process until they are coarsely chopped.

Yield: 1 9-inch pie
Prep Time: 15 minutes
Total Time: 1 hour

Crust:
- **1 cup quinoa flour**
- **⅛ tsp. salt**

1. Preheat oven to 350°F.
2. Combine the quinoa flour and salt.
3. In a separate bowl, combine the boiling water with the walnut oil and beat with a whisk or in the blender until white and frothy. Add to flour mixture. Stir to incorporate all the liquid.

¼ cup boiling water
¼ cup walnut oil

Filling:
¼ cup unsalted butter, at room temperature
1 cup maple syrup
3 eggs
2 tsp. vanilla
½ tsp. salt
1½ cups coarsely chopped walnuts

4. Press into an oiled, shallow, 9-inch pie plate.
5. Whip the butter until creamy. Add the maple syrup, eggs, vanilla, and salt. Beat again. Stir in the walnuts and pour into the unbaked pie shell.
6. Bake 45 to 50 minutes or until a knife inserted in the center comes out clean. Cool.

Pumpkin Cheesecake with Quinoa Ginger Crust

Some pumpkin pies are creamier than others, I have reversed the usual proportions to create a silky pumpkin pie—mostly cream but unmistakably pumpkin. Preparation time does not include licking the bowl.

Prep Tip: Bake one small sugar or "pie" pumpkin in a 375°F. oven for 45 minutes, or until it is soft throughout. Cool to room temperature. Cut in half, remove seeds and scoop out pulp. Purée the pulp in a food mill, processor, or blender.

Yield: 1 9-inch cheesecake
Prep Time: 30 minutes using prepared pumpkin purée
Total Time: 1 ½ hours

Crust:
1½ cups quinoa flour
1 tsp. ginger powder
⅛ tsp. salt
½ cup unsalted butter
¼ cup clover honey

Filling:
1 lb. cream cheese, softened
3 egg yolks
3 eggs
1 cup pumpkin purée
¾ cup clover honey
1 tsp. nutmeg

Edging:
¼ cup clover honey
½ cup blanched, ground almonds

1. Preheat oven to 325°F.
2. Combine the quinoa flour, ginger, and salt. Using a pastry cutter, two knives, or a food processor, cut butter into the flour mixture. Add the honey and mix. Press into the bottom of a buttered 9-inch springform pan.
3. Using a food processor or mixer, combine the cream cheese, egg yolks, eggs, pumpkin purée, honey and nutmeg. Pour onto the unbaked crust. Bake for 1 hour or until center is firm. Cool. Remove sides of pan.
4. Heat the honey. Using a knife, spread honey on the sides of cake and press almonds into sides.

Variations:
- Substitute maple syrup for honey.
- Top with additional blanched ground almonds.
- Substitute yogurt for the pumpkin purée.

Minted Quinoa Layered with Date Sugar

This pudding is the inspiration of my friend, Barbara Svenning, who develops recipes for natural food companies. In her words, "One day I was searching for something a little special to enjoy with a cup of mint tea. I sprinkled date sugar and cinnamon over cooked quinoa and presto—one of my favorite quinoa desserts was born."

Yield: 4 servings
Prep Time: 15 minutes
Total Time: 1 ½ hours

1 cup mint tea
few grains of salt
½ cup quinoa
½ cup date sugar
2 tsp. cinnamon
8 to 12 Medjool or Deglit Noor dates

1. Bring the tea and salt to a boil, add the quinoa, reduce heat, cover, and cook over low heat for 15 minutes. Remove from heat and allow to rest, covered, for 5 to 10 minutes. Fluff with a fork.
2. Meanwhile, combine the date sugar and cinnamon and place 1 teaspoon of the mixture in each of 4 8-ounce custard cups.
3. While the quinoa is still hot, spoon 2 tablespoons into each custard cup and gently but firmly press flat. Sprinkle each cup with an additional 2 teaspoons sugar mixture, and cover with another 2 tablespoons hot quinoa. Cover with remaining sugar mixture. Cool completely (about 1 hour). Quinoa may be covered and refrigerated at this point, or unmolded onto plates and served with 2 or 3 dates.

Variations:
- Alternate layers in parfait or wine glasses and serve warm; top with whipped cream.
- Substitute cocoa powder mixed with natural sugar for the date sugar mixture.
- Substitute fruit preserves for the date sugar mixture.
- Add ground walnuts to the cooked quinoa.
- Substitute milk for the mint tea, using a double boiler to cook the quinoa.

Felipe Rojas-Lombardi's Quinoa Rum Pudding

This exceedingly rich pudding is best made on a nippy day when it is good to settle down close to the stove. Pull up a stool and read a good mystery while stirring—as the plot thickens so does the pudding. After this pudding has been thoroughly cooled at room temperature, it can be covered and stored in the refrigerator for several days.

Yield: 6 servings
Prep Time: 1 hour
Total Time: 1½ hours

½ cup dark rum
½ cup raisins
3 cups cooked quinoa
1 cup milk
1 cup heavy cream
1 cup natural sugar
¼ tsp. salt
½ tsp. cinnamon
⅛ tsp. ground cloves
¼ cup grated fresh coconut (optional)
2 egg yolks
powdered cinnamon

1. Mix the raisins with the rum and set aside.
2. Meanwhile, in the top portion of a large, non-aluminum double boiler, place the quinoa, milk, cream, sugar, salt, cinnamon and cloves. Simmer over boiling water for 30 minutes or until most of the liquid has evaporated and the mixture is thick.
3. Stir in the raisins, rum and coconut. Mix and continue cooking for an additional 5 to 10 minutes, until all of the moisture has evaporated and the spoon leaves a path when moved across the bottom of the pan.
4. Remove from heat. While beating continuously and vigorously, add the egg yolks. Continue beating until the yolks are thoroughly absorbed. Pour pudding into a shallow dish. Sprinkle with powdered cinnamon. Allow to cool thoroughly at room temperature.

Apricot-Quinoa "Tapioca"

For many, tapioca evokes childhood memories of that pearly, yet soothingly smooth dessert. Quinoa "tapioca" is texturally similar, but in nutritional value and flavor it far surpasses highly refined tapioca. Dried apricots and hazelnuts add character and sophistication to this simple pudding.

Yield: 4 to 6 servings
Prep Time: 5 minutes, using cooked quinoa
Total Time: 3 hours

1 cup dried apricots
1 Tbsp. quinoa (or white unbleached) flour
2 cups milk
3 cups cooked quinoa
⅓ cup maple syrup
2 eggs, beaten
1 tsp. vanilla
¼ tsp. salt
½ cup chopped hazelnuts
½ tsp. cinnamon
¼ tsp. nutmeg

1. Toss the apricots with the flour. Place them in a processor and process until they are chopped fine.
2. Heat the milk and apricot pieces in a small saucepan. Allow to stand for 30 minutes or until the apricots are softened.
3. Preheat oven to 350°F.
4. Combine the apricot mixture with the quinoa, maple syrup, eggs, vanilla, and salt. Place in an oiled shallow baking dish. Sprinkle hazelnuts, cinnamon, and nutmeg on top. Bake for 45 minutes or until the liquid is absorbed.

Variations:
- Substitute dried peaches, apples, and/or pears for the apricots.
- Instead of baking, cook in the top of a double boiler.

Papaya-Quinoa Pudding

There are days when I want something more elaborate than fresh fruit for dessert, but I want that something to be absolutely wholesome. This pudding fulfills both those requirements so expertly that guests of all dietary persuasions are enchanted. The star anise imparts an authentic South American flavor.

Prep Tip: Assemble the pudding just prior to serving. If assembled several hours in advance, the papaya enzymes cause the pudding to run. At high elevations, cook the quinoa over direct heat and stir frequently.

Yield: **4 servings**
Time: **30 minutes, using cooked quinoa**

½ cup quinoa
2 cups vanilla soymilk
¼ cup maple syrup
1 Tbsp. agar-agar flakes
2 whole star anise
few grains of salt
1 Tbsp. tahini
1 Tbsp. kuzu, dissolved in 1½ Tbsp. cool water
1 small, fully ripe papaya
1 tsp. fresh lime juice
¼ cup natural sugar

1. Place the quinoa, soymilk, maple syrup, agar-agar flakes, and star anise in the top of a double boiler. Cover and cook over boiling water for 30 minutes. Remove the star anise. Add the tahini and the dissolved kuzu and, stirring continuously, continue to cook for 2 minutes.
2. Meanwhile, peel and seed the papaya. Cut it into small, thin slices and toss with lime juice and all but 1 teaspoon of the natural sugar. Set aside.
3. Pour the quinoa mixture into a blender and blend until smooth. Chill until cool. Layer papaya slices and pudding into 4 parfait glasses, beginning with a layer of papaya and ending with a layer of pudding. Sprinkle the tops with the remaining sugar.

Variations:
- Substitute a 2-inch cinnamon stick or 3 drops of anise extract for the star anise.
- Use chocolate- or carob-flavored soymilk and add 1 tablespoon grain coffee.
- Substitute blueberries, cherimoya, mango, pepino, raspberries, or strawberries for the papaya.

Burnt Orange-Pistachio Swirls

This fragrant cookie has a crisp edge and moist interior. Its intriguing flavor makes it perfect for holiday gift-giving—as well as for tea time, lunch boxes, desserts and after-school snacks.

Prep Tip: Use a vegetable peeler to remove thin strips of rind from oranges, and use organic oranges if available.

Yield: 24 2 ½-inch cookies
Prep Time: 45 minutes
Total Time: 1 hour

thin strips of peel from 6 medium oranges
1 cup unsalted pistachio nuts, in the shell
¼ pound unsalted butter, softened
⅔ cup maple syrup
1 cup quinoa flour
½ cup whole wheat pastry flour
1 tsp. baking powder
¼ tsp. salt

1. Place the orange peel on a baking sheet and bake in a 250°F. oven for 25 minutes, or until crisp and lightly browned.
2. Meanwhile, shell pistachio nuts by holding each on a cutting board between thumb and forefinger. Place knife blade where the shell splits and slice down to open shell. Reserve 24 of the best-looking halves (bright green and unbroken). Finely chop the remaining nuts.
3. Grind the toasted orange peel in the blender until fine.
4. Cream together the butter and maple syrup.
5. In a separate bowl, combine the quinoa flour, whole wheat pastry flour, baking powder, salt, and the ground orange peel.
6. Preheat oven to 350°F.
7. Add the creamed butter and syrup to the flour mixture. Stir in the chopped nuts. Press mixture through a pastry tube onto an oiled baking sheet to form 24 swirled rounds. Press 2 of the reserved pistachio nuts into each cookie.
8. Bake about 12 minutes, or until very lightly browned at edges and on bottom.

Variations:

- Substitute almonds, cashews, filberts, or peanuts for the pistachios.
- Place dough in a plastic bag, shape into a log, and freeze to slice and bake at another time.
- Drop by tablespoons onto baking sheets, top with whole or chopped nuts, and bake.

Mocha Almond Sandwich Cookies

The heady aroma of toasted almonds makes this an outstanding cookie for adult tastes; and the rich mocha icing tranforms it into a drawing-room delicacy.

Prep Tip: The dough may be prepared up to 5 days in advance. The cookies may be baked and iced 2 to 3 days ahead. Layer, with waxed paper between the layers, and store at room temperature in an airtight container.

Yield: 18 2-inch filled cookies
Prep Time: 45 minutes

1. Cream the butter with the sugar.
2. Toast the almonds in a 250°F. oven for 10 to 15 minutes. Finely grind the nuts in a food proces-

Total Time: 1 hour, 10 minutes

3/4 cup unsalted butter
1/3 cup natural sugar
1 cup almonds
1 cup quinoa flour
1 cup unbleached white flour
1/4 tsp. salt
1/4 tsp. vanilla

Icing:
1 oz. unsweetened chocolate
2 tsp. unsalted butter
1/8 cup strong coffee
3/4 cup natural sugar
1/2 tsp. vanilla
1/8 tsp. salt

sor or nut grinder. Add the flours, ground almonds, salt, and vanilla to butter mixture and stir just until dough comes together. Gather dough into a ball.

3. Preheat oven to 350°F.

4. Roll the dough between sheets of waxed paper to a 1/4-inch thickness. Cut into 2-inch rounds with a fluted cutter. Place on an oiled cookie sheet and bake until lightly colored, about 7 to 10 minutes. Remove to a rack and cool cookies completely.

5. To make the icing, combine the chocolate, butter, coffee, sugar, vanilla, and salt in top of a double boiler. Cook over hot water, stirring as necessary until smooth. Line another baking sheet with waxed paper. Spread the flat side of 1 cookie with a thin chocolate coating. Sandwich with the flat side of a second cookie. Place on a prepared baking sheet. Repeat with remaining cookies and chocolate. Dip a fork in remaining chocolate and drizzle lines over each cookie in decorative pattern. Let stand at cool room temperature until chocolate sets.

Variations:

- Substitute 1 teaspoon grain coffee and 1/8 cup water for the coffee.
- Substitute hazelnuts for the almonds.
- Add a drop of mint extract to the icing.

Pfeffernüsse

Pfeffernüsse, literally "pepper nuts" in German, are traditional anise-flavored cookies that really do contain pepper. There are numerous pfeffernüsse recipes, but this one seems to be the simplest and most healthful. It requires no refined sweeteners, butter, eggs, leavening, or wheat.

Prep Tip: Prepare oat flour in blender using 1/2 cup rolled oats.

Yield: 24 1-inch cookies
Time: 30 minutes

1 cup quinoa flour
1/4 tsp. white pepper
1/8 tsp. salt
1/4 cup almond oil

1. Preheat oven to 350°F.
2. In a mixing bowl, combine quinoa flour, pepper, and salt.
3. Using a fork or whisk, combine the oil, honey, anise extract and vanilla.
4. Add wet ingredients to dry. Mix well. Shape into 1-inch balls. Roll balls in oat flour. Place on

1/4 cup clover honey
1/2 tsp. anise extract
1/2 tsp. vanilla
oat flour for dusting

an oiled baking sheet, and bake for 15 minutes.

Variations:

- Substitute ginger powder for the pepper, and molasses for a small part of the honey.
- Push the dough through a pastry tube to form fancy wreaths or rosettes.
- Shape the dough into a log shape, wrap in plastic, and freeze or refrigerate to bake at another time.
- Substitute almond extract for the anise extract and omit the pepper; shape into 2-inch balls, flatten on a baking sheet, and press a whole almond into each cookie.

Scottish Shortbread

Simple, rich, and satisfying, Scottish shortbread moves uptown when made with quinoa flour. This shortbread needs no accompaniment—which does not mean that you cannot serve it with a dish of peach ice cream, alongside fresh cherimoya, or on a tray with dessert cheeses.

Yield: 2 8-inch flat round breads
Prep Time: 10 minutes
Total Time: 30 minutes

1/2 cup unsalted butter
1/2 cup natural sugar, sifted
1/2 tsp. vanilla
1 1/4 cups quinoa flour
1/8 tsp. salt

1. Preheat oven to 350°F.
2. Cream the butter, sugar, and vanilla.
3. Sift together the flour and salt and stir into the butter mixture. Mix just until the dough comes together. Press the dough into 2 8-inch rounds and flute the edges. Prick dough well. Bake 20 minutes or until slightly browned. Cut each round into 8 wedges while still warm.

Variations:

- Add 1/2 cup unsweetened coconut.
- Chill dough. Roll out and cut into shapes.
- Press hulled sesame seeds into the rounds before baking.

Macadamia Bars

These mouth-watering sweets are a variation of the Southern pecan bar. If unshelled macadamia nuts are available, find a very hard surface you do not mind marring, get yourself a hammer, take a good aim, and you will soon have a treat.

Prep Tip: For the base, prepare one recipe of Scottish Shortbread dough (see preceding recipe) in advance.

Yield: About 3 dozen 1 ½ by 3-inch bars
Prep Time: 15 minutes, using prepared shortbread dough
Total Time: 55 minutes

Macadamia Topping:
1½ cups natural sugar, shifted
2 Tbsp. quinoa flour
½ tsp. baking powder
¼ tsp. salt
2 eggs, lightly beaten
1 Tbsp. Grand Marnier
1 tsp. vanilla
1½ cups macadamia nuts, chopped

1. Preheat oven to 350°F.
2. Pat shortbread dough into a 9 by 12-inch pan. Bake for 15 minutes.
3. Meanwhile, combine the sugar, flour, baking powder, and salt. Add the eggs, Grand Marnier, and vanilla. Mix just enough to blend.
4. Spread the macadamia nuts over the shortbread, which has baked for 15 minutes. Pour and spread the sugar topping. Return to the hot oven and bake for an additional 15 minutes or until the cookies are lightly browned. Cool, then slice into bar shapes.

Variations:
- Substitute pine nuts or Brazil nuts for the macadamias.
- Substitute 3/4 cup raspberry jam for 3/4 cup sugar.

Dried Fruit and Walnut Quinoa Bars

The just-baked aroma of these old-fashioned bars is nearly overwhelming. Quinoa flour heightens the fruit and nut flavors to an extraordinary degree.

Prep Tip: Dough may be made 2 to 48 hours in advance. To maintain the bars' freshness for up to a week, cool, cut, and store in an airtight container.

Yield: 24 1½ by 2-inch bars
Prep Time: 10 minutes
Total Time: 50 minutes

2 cups quinoa flour
⅛ tsp. salt
½ cup pitted prunes
½ cup dried apricots
½ cup dried apple slices
½ cup dates
¾ cup chopped walnuts
½ cup raisins
2 cups quinoa flour
⅛ tsp. salt

1. Preheat oven to 350°F.
2. In a mixing bowl, combine the quinoa flour with the salt. Coarsely chop the prunes, apricots, apples, dates and walnuts. Add the raisins and chopped fruits and nuts to the flour mixture. Toss to blend.
3. Combine the maple syrup, oil, applesauce, and vanilla. Fold into the flour mixture. Spread batter into an oiled 11 by 7-inch baking pan with a narrow rim. Bake until light brown and a toothpick inserted in the center comes out clean, about 40 minutes. Remove from oven. Cool at room temperature and cut into bars.

⅔ cup maple syrup
½ cup safflower oil
½ cup unsweetened applesauce
½ tsp. vanilla

Hermits

Those who do not like very sweet spice cookies may skip these. The rest of us will delight in their triple sweetness (from natural sugar, molasses, and currants) and moist, nutty texture.

Yield: 24 2 ½-inch cookies
Prep Time: 10 minutes
Total Time: 25 minutes

2 cups quinoa flour
1 tsp. cinnamon
½ tsp. nutmeg
½ tsp. ground cloves
¼ tsp. salt
2 tsp. baking powder
2 eggs, lightly beaten
½ cup safflower oil
1 cup natural sugar, sifted
¼ cup molasses
¾ cup walnuts, chopped
1 cup currants

1. Preheat oven to 350°F.
2. In a mixing bowl, combine the flour, cinnamon, nutmeg, cloves, salt, and baking powder.
3. Combine the eggs, oil, natural sugar, and molasses. Add wet ingredients to dry ingredients. Stir in the walnuts and currants. Drop by spoonfuls onto an oiled baking sheet. Bake for 15 minutes.

Variations:

- Substitute raisins, chopped apricots, chopped dates, or sultanas for the currants.
- Add 1 teaspoon ground ginger; place in an oiled pan and bake in a 350°F. oven for 30 to 35 minutes.

Hazelnut Cookies

These aromatic cookies contain only a few ingredients—but each ingredient has ample flavor. Tuck hazelnut cookies into lunch boxes or serve with hot or ice tea.

Prep Tip: Cookies may be made up to one week in advance, cooled thoroughly, and stored in an airtight container. Cookie dough may be made several days in advance and kept refrigerated.

Yield: 24 3-inch cookies
Prep Time: 25 minutes
Total Time: 30 minutes

⅔ cup unsalted butter
⅓ cup natural sugar
½ tsp. vanilla

1. Preheat oven to 375°F.
2. In food processor, cream together the butter, sugar, vanilla, and almond extract.
3. Add the flour, hazelnuts, and salt, then process until the dough forms into a ball. Using your hands, form into 2-inch round balls and place on an oiled cookie sheet. Dip the bottom of a drink-

2 drops almond extract
$1\frac{1}{4}$ cups quinoa flour
$1\frac{1}{4}$ cups ground hazelnuts
$\frac{1}{4}$ tsp. salt
$\frac{1}{4}$ cup natural sugar for dusting

ing glass into the sugar. Flatten each ball with the sugared glass bottom. Bake for 10 to 12 minutes or just until browned.

Variations:

- Substitute walnuts, pine nuts, almonds or coconut for the hazelnuts.
- Substitute 1/3 cup tahini and 1/3 cup oil for the butter.

Peanut-Protein Wafers

The freshest peanut butter makes the tastiest cookies, so why not make the peanut butter at the same time as the dough? This is the quintessential after-school snack, sweet, chewy, and healthful.

Yield: 24 $2\frac{1}{2}$-inch cookies
Time: 30 minutes

2 cups roasted, unsalted peanuts
1 cup natural sugar
2 eggs
1 tsp. vanilla
1 cup quinoa flour
$\frac{1}{4}$ tsp. salt

1. Preheat oven to 350°F.
2. In a food processor, process the peanuts until they turn into peanut butter. Add the natural sugar, eggs, and vanilla and process to blend.
3. In a mixing bowl, combine the quinoa flour and salt. Add the peanut butter mixture and stir, then knead lightly with hands. Shape into 24 1 1/2-inch balls and lay on oiled baking sheets. With a moistened fork, flatten into 2 1/2-inch cookies. Bake 15 minutes.

Variations:

- Shape half of the dough into a log 2 1/2-inches in diameter. Wrap in plastic and refrigerate or freeze to slice and bake at another time.
- Substitute cashews for peanuts.

PART III

APPENDIXES

A. How to Grow, Harvest, and Winnow Quinoa

Unlike most grains, quinoa is practical to grow at home because it needs little attention and no specialized equipment for harvesting or hulling. It also provides tasty greens in early summer, delicious young seed heads in mid-summer, and it is a beautiful garden plant. Growing this ancient grain enables you to enjoy varieties—each with its own unique flavor profile—which are not commercially available.

Obtain seed-quality quinoa from one of the sources listed below. (The germination rate of quinoa available in food stores is sporadic due to saponin removal techniques.) Quinoa grows in cool dry regions where temperatures do not exceed 85 degrees F. Optimum rain fall or irrigation is between 15 and 20 inches during the growing season. Any standing water kills quinoa. Excessive water produces tall plants which easily lodge and break.

Sow quinoa in the spring when the soil is warm. Seeds should be set about one-half inch deep with four plants per foot on twenty-inch rows. A precision vegetable planter facilitates planting. Quinoa responds to nitrogen-rich soils. If the seedlings dry out before roots are sunk, the young plants will die. A large number of insects favor the plants at all stages and birds feed on the mature seed.

Maturity in the high Colorado mountains comes in 90 to 120 days. With cloudier weather or less intense sun, maturity takes longer. Under good conditions the seed heads in the soft dough stage are intensely colored. As the seeds reach the hard dough stage their colors fade.

To harvest quinoa wait until the plant is thoroughly dry. Cut the stalks. Grasp the base of a stalk with one hand and hold it over a wide container (like a bucket or bag). Run your other hand along the stalk and strip the seeds into the container.

Rub seed heads between both hands to separate the grain from the chaff. Pick out large leaf and stalk pieces. Now it is ready to winnow. Here are two winnowing methods: Wait until there is a light breeze. Place grain in a wide bowl or tray. Toss the grain up into the air and catch it in the bowl. The chaff blows away. A second winnowing technique is to spread a tarp in front of a fan. Slowly pour the grain into the air current. The chaff blows away and the seeds fall onto the tarp.

Once harvested, the seeds should be kept exceptionally dry. If exposed to moisture—even on the stalk in the field—they sprout. It is most convenient to wash seeds *only* as needed and just prior to use. If extra seeds are washed, immediately dry them to prevent sprouting.

A small quantity of quinoa seed for planting is available free from:

Dr. Duane Johnson
Department of Agronomy
Colorado State University
Fort Collins, CO 80523

Several different quinoa strains may be purchased from:

Abundant Life Seed Foundation
Box 772
Port Townsend, WA 98368
Send $1.00 for their seed catalog

Talavaya
Box 2
Tesuque Drive
Espanola, NM 87532

For information about farming quinoa contact:

Dr. John McCamant
Sierra Blanca
2650 S. Jackson
Denver, CO 80210

Whole quinoa and quinoa products (including flour, pasta, tempeh, and baked goods) are sold in natural food stores, speciality food stores, and in some supermarkets. If quinoa is not available in your favorite store, contact one of the following companies. These companies market quinoa nationally and will inform you of your nearest quinoa retailer.

Arrowhead Mills
Box 2049
Herford, TX 79045
806 364–0730

Eden Foods
701 Tecumseh Road
Clinton, MI 59236
313 973–9400

Quinoa Corporation
24248 Crenshaw Blvd., Suite 220
Torrence, CA90505
213 530–8666

B. How to Sprout Quinoa

Quinoa sprouts are similar to alfalfa sprouts in appearance and use. Sprouts made from colored seed varieties have beautiful red stems which give this sprout a stand-out appearance. Sometimes saponin-free seed will sprout, but for consistent results use seed-quality quinoa. (Seed sources listed in Appendix A.)

To make a quart of quinoa sprouts, place two tablespoons of seed in a quart jar. Soak for four to eight hours. Place a piece of cheesecloth or nylon over the jar's mouth. Secure with a rubber band or screw-on jar ring. Drain out the water and allow the jar to stand, inverted, in a dish-drainer or propped at an angle on your counter. Rinse the sprouts with fresh water several times a day.

The sprouts will be ready in four to six days, or when two-inches long and with bright green leaves. Use in salads and on sandwiches. Quinoa sprouts hold well in the refrigerator for a week.

C. Quinoa Flour

Whole grain flours have ample flavor but yield heavy products. White flour imparts a light, delicate crumb but is short on flavor and nutrients. Happily, quinoa flour combines the best features of both.

Quinoa flour is the lightest of all flours, making it a superior choice for many fine pastries. Its unique crumb is tender, moist and delicate. Quinoa flour increases a product's flavor range and depth, and contributes even more nutrients than does whole wheat flour.

Fruitcakes, cookies, pancakes, and waffles are improved by using up to 100 percent quinoa flour. And because it is gluten-free, quinoa flour is best combined with wheat for leavened bread, biscuits, finely textured cakes, rolled pie crust, crêpes, tortillas, and pasta.

Quinoa flour is quickly and easily made at home. As quinoa is a much softer grain than wheat, rice, or corn, it pulverizes in a few minutes. For super-fine, powdery flour, use a grain mill. (Cooks who favor whole grain flours will find a home grain mill an extremely useful acquisition.) A nut grinder, food blender, or coffee mill will suffice, but will produce a beady flour. Fortunately, even coarsely ground quinoa flour works well in most recipes. For pastries demanding a very fine texture, use fine quinoa flour. Following are the proportions of grain to flour:

QUINOA	*QUINOA FLOUR*
1/3 cup	1/2 cup
2/3 cup	3/4 cup
3/4 cup	1 cup
1 cup minus 1 tablespoon	1 1/4 cups
1 cup plus 2 tablespoons	1 1/2 cups
1 1/4 cups	1 3/4 cups
1 1/2 cups	2 cups

A distinct advantage of homemade quinoa flour (blended or milled) is that you can make it as needed. Fresh flour is more delicious and healthful, and it imparts more energy. Once milled, the oils in all whole grain flours start to oxidize and become rancid. Rancidity is associated with free radicals, carcinogens, and the aging process. As quinoa is richer in oils than cereal grains, its flour is even more prone to rancidity. Grind whole grain flours only as they are needed.

If you purchase quinoa flour—or any whole grain flour—store it, covered, in a cool, dark place to help maintain its freshness. It is advisable to purchase only freshly ground flour and to use it within one month of purchase. Whole grain flour over a month old is better for your compost heap than your cookies.

D. Chilies

The sweet *Capsicum* vegetables, such as bell peppers, are termed peppers in this book. Their hot, pungent relatives are termed chilies. Hundreds of different chili varieties exist and their multiple names vary from region to region. To compound the confusion, new varieties frequently appear on the market. Hopefully your greengrocer is chili-wise and can help you select them according to the degree of hotness that you desire.

Capsaicin is an oily substance found in fresh chilies which may literally burn the skin, especially the eyes, nose and lips. Nearly 90 percent of the capsaicin is concentrated in the membranes of chilies, so depending upon the chili "temperature" you desire, you may wish to exclude, or include, these parts. Below is a list of the chilies used in this book. But first, here are preparation tips for fresh chilies:

Wear plastic or rubber gloves when you handle chilies, or immediately wash your hands thoroughly with soap and water afterwards. A chili is peeled prior to use. First slit the skin near the stem. Next place it in a broiler pan about four inches from the heat source and broil until the skin blisters, from 5 to 15 minutes per side. Or, blister a chili by holding it, with tongs, over a gas flame.

Once blistered, immediately place the chili in a tightly covered container (or wrap in a brown paper bag) and allow it to steam for 15 minutes. Then its skin is easily slipped off. Remove chili skin, seeds, (membranes if you wish to reduce capsaicin), and stem under cold running water to protect your skin from being burned.

Anaheim The Anaheim is a mildly hot chili pepper which is bright green when young and deepens to red at maturity. It is the longest of chilies (up to eight inches) and is available year round in many regions.

Ancho The word "ancho" typically refers to a dried *poblano* chili. (In some regions it also refers to a fresh chili.) In this book the ancho is used dried; it is generally mild-flavored.

Fresno The firey hot Fresno is best identified by comparing it to the better known jalapeño. The Fresno is a little larger (but broader at the stem-end and more pointed at the tip) than the jalapeño, it is lighter in color, and it is equally as hot.

Jalapeño One of the hottest chilies, the small dark-green jalapeño, is one- to three-inches long, blunt at the end and smooth-skinned. It is available twelve months of the year.

Poblano The poblano is a mildly hot Mexican chili which is at peak in the late summer and fall. It is typically about five inches long and looks like an elongated bell pepper. It ranges in color from dark green to almost black with red spots.

Serrano This searing chili (from one- to two-inches long and no more than 1-inch wide) looks innocuous, but is not. The serrano ranges from orange to green in color and may be used raw or roasted.

E. Natural Sugar

By law any substance labeled sugar must be refined to at least 96 percent pure sucrose. This includes Turbinado, "raw," brown, and yellow sugar. When cane or beets are refined to this degree of purity their resulting flavor is harsh and one-dimensional.

Cane sugar which does not meet the Food and Drug Administration's Purity Code cannot be called "sugar." There are at least three lightly refined cane sweeteners on the market which have their mineral content intact and therefore contain under 96 percent sucrose. These products have a well-rounded, multi-dimensional sweetness. They impart to baked goods the inimitable "sugar" crumb. They are:

- Sucanat—made from organic cane and is labeled "dehydrated cane juice." It is available in gourmet and natural food stores.
- Piloncillo—a Mexican cane product available in Southwestern supermarkets and Latin food markets. It comes in hard cone shapes and must be dissolved in water prior to use. (Do NOT try to blend piloncillo cones for they can cause the blender glass to shatter. Trying to chop these cones with a knife is perilous to finger tips.)
- Jaggery—an imported, unrefined cane sugar available in Indian and Middle Eastern markets.

When dry, Sucanat and jaggery become lumpy. If simple sifting does not eliminate the lumps, then blending quickly reduces them to a fine powder.

In any recipe, you may substitute natural sugar for refined sugar cup-for-cup. Expect a less intense—but more satisfying—sweetness.

If you adapt a recipe which calls for any sugar with a liquid natural sweetener (such as maple syrup, honey, or rice syrup), then reduce the liquid measurements accordingly.

Glossary

Aburage Also called *age*, this deep-fried tofu has a tender, meat-like texture. Aburage is available at Oriental and natural food stores. To make it at home, press out excess water from tofu slices and deep-fry in 375°F. oil until golden brown.

Agar This mineral-rich seaweed makes an excellent gel which sets more quickly than does gelatin. Agar flakes or *kanten* bars substitute for agar. They are available in natural or Oriental food stores.

Anasazi beans Mottled purple and white, these flavorful beans are an heirloom seed which have remained a favorite of the Pueblo Indians for centuries. Anasazi are available in regional and natural food stores.

Annato A common food coloring in butter, margarine, cheese, confections, and South American ethnic foods comes from the salmon-red annato seed. These seeds are available in Latin, natural, and specialty food stores.

Arrowroot flour The root of the tropical arrowroot plant yields a fine-grained starch which makes a superior and more healthful thickener than highly refined cornstarch. Substitute arrowroot flour, measure for measure, for cornstarch. In sauces, dissolve it in cold water prior to use. Arrowroot flour is available in natural food stores and some supermarkets.

Black sesame seeds For the most hearty sesame flavor use black sesame seeds. Purchase only those seeds which are mottled with varying shades of browns and blacks. A monochromatic black color indicates that they are dyed. Black sesame seeds are available in Oriental and natural food markets.

Bolita beans A favorite bean in Mexican and southwestern cuisine is the bolita. Their great variation in size, shape, and their rose-to-tan colors reveal that they are not hybridized. Bolitas are available in natural food stores and southwestern markets.

Brown rice vinegar This mildly acidic vinegar is available in gourmet and natural food stores. It has 5 percent acidity or less and is reputed for its culinary and medicinal properties. Other vinegars, including distilled, cider, malt, and wine vinegar, range from 40 to 60 percent acetic acid.

Buttermilk Commercial buttermilk is pasteurized skim milk which is inoculated with a lactic acid culture and contains stabilizers. Real buttermilk is the byproduct of butter making. You may subsitute yogurt for buttermilk; or you may make "buttermilk" by adding one tablespoon of lemon juice (or vinegar) to one cup of milk or soymilk. Stir the milk and let it stand for 10 minutes or until it clabbers.

Chilies *See* Appendix D.

Date sugar This coarse "sugar" is made of pitted, dehydrated, and pulverized dates. It is as nutrient-rich as are the dates from which it is made and it tastes both sugary and date-like. Available at natural food stores, store date sugar in a cool place.

Dulse The best food source of iron, the seaweed dulse is typically harvested in Nova Scotia and Maine as well as in the Puget Sound area. It is available in natural food stores.

Eggs For the best flavor use *fresh* organic eggs from grain-fed, free-running chickens. Refrigerate eggs in a covered container and use within a week.

Garbanzo flour Also known as chick-pea, besan, or gram flour. Garbanzo flour is made from finely milled and then roasted garbanzos. It is available in East Indian, Middle Eastern and natural foods markets.

Ghee Similar to clarified butter, ghee is pure butterfat and is ideal for sautéing or frying. When cooking it emits a wonderful aroma and imbues foods with a nutty and sweet flavor characteristic of East Indian cookery.

Ginger juice Here is how to extract one teaspoon of ginger juice: Take a knob of fresh ginger root the size of a small walnut, and scrape off its skin. Next, finely grate the ginger onto a saucer. Squeeze the ginger pulp to extract the juice.

Grain coffee There are numerous beverages available which approximate the aroma and flavor of coffee but are free of tannin and caffeine. They are typically made of malted barley and flavored with other grains, vegetables, fruits, sweeteners, or herbs. Most supermarkets carry at least one variety; natural food stores carry a larger selection.

Kombu seaweed This amazing sea vegetable tenderizes foods and enhances flavors with its natural glutamic acid. A mineral-rich food, kombu makes "instant" soup stock. It is available in Oriental or natural food markets and in the health sections of some supermarkets.

Kuzu The starch-like extract of a root, *kuzu* is used as a thickener like cornstarch or arrowroot flour. In Japanese and macrobiotic cookery it is highly prized for its subtle flavor, as well as its culinary and medicinal uses.

Liquid smoke Several varieties of liquid smoke are available in supermarkets. Favor a natural brand which is made by burning wood, condensing the smoke, and then filtering the liquid until it is free of polycyclic aromatic hydrocarbons.

Mirin This Japanese "cooking wine" is similar to *saké*. Authentic, natural *mirin* is made only of sweet rice, rice *koji*, and water. A less costly variety may contain salt. Avoid mirin which contains refined sweeteners. Mirin is available in Oriental markets, and some gourmet and natural food stores.

Miso This protein-rich fermented soybean purée is typically used as a soup base, but has numerous other food applications. Originally a Japanese staple, miso has secured a niche in healthy American cuisine. Domestically made miso appeals more to American tastes as it is lighter in flavor and salt content. Miso is available in Oriental and natural food stores.

Mochi A delicacy made of pounded sweet rice, *mochi* may be made of either whole or refined sweet rice. It is available in Oriental and natural food markets.

Natural sugar *See* Appendix E.

Natural soy sauce Natural soy sauce contains only soybeans, wheat, salt, and water and is aged for at least one year. It has a wide range of rounded flavors which enables it to season many foods with less sodium than if only salt were used. Commercial soy sauce is made in a few days using chemically extracted soy and numerous additives. It has a harsh and one-dimensional flavor.

Nori seaweed Paper-thin and black, *nori* is best known as a sushi wrapper. Nori is rich in calcium and protein and has more vitamin A than carrots. It is available in Oriental, specialty, and natural food markets.

Nori flakes Flaked nori (not flavored nori condiments) is sometimes available in natural and Oriental food stores. If you don't find it, tear several sheets of nori into pieces and blend in a thoroughly dried blender.

Nutritional yeast This nutrient-rich additive is used for its high nutrient profile and also because it imparts a rich, cheese-like flavor. Nutritional yeast is available in health food and natural food stores.

Pickled ginger Pungent pickled ginger, without sugar or additives, is available in natural food stores.

Posole Whole white corn is parched in lime water and dried. Unlike untreated dried corn, it may be cooked whole. Posole has a delicately sweet flavor. It is available in natural food stores and Hispanic markets.

Quinoa flour *See* Appendix C.

Rice syrup Made from cooked rice and enzymes, rice syrup is high in maltose and, according to macrobiotic cookery, is the most healthful sweetener. Rice syrup is suitable for some diabetics. It has a honeylike consistency but a much lighter taste. Rice syrup is available in natural food stores.

Roasted sesame oil When it is cooking, roasted sesame oil is highly aromatic and imparts a characteristic Oriental flavor to foods. Available in many grades, the better oils are made from mechanically pressed sesame seeds which have been hand-toasted and filtered. Roasted sesame oil is available in natural and Oriental food markets.

Salt Commercial salt is highly refined (97.5% NaCl) and has an abrasive taste which burns the tongue and leaves a harsh and metallic aftertaste. Additive-free sea salt is as equally refined as is commercial salt. For the best-tasting food, use natural sea salt, which is rich in trace minerals and contains less than 97.5% NaCl. Such salt has a smooth and mellow salt flavor with a sweet aftertaste. It is available in natural food stores.

Seitan Also known as *kofu* or wheat meat, seitan is a seasoned wheat gluten which has a texture and flavor reminiscent of meat. Substitute it freely for any meat. Seitan has regional availablity in natural food stores, or it may be made at home.

Soba A hearty and flavorful Japanese buckwheat pasta which may, or may not, also contain wheat. Available in Oriental and specialty food markets.

Soymilk This highly popular and healthful beverage approximates the flavor of milk. It may be substituted, measure for measure, for milk. Soymilk contains approximately one-third the fat, fewer calories, no cholesterol, and 15 times as much iron as cow's milk. It is now available in many supermarkets as well as natural food stores.

Tahini A Middle Eastern style purée made of hulled sesame seeds. Distinctive tasting and protein-rich, tahini is widely available in specialty and ethnic food markets.

Tamari A quality natural soy sauce made without wheat and aged for at least one year. Low-sodium varieties are also available. Tamari is found in natural food stores and the natural food sections of some supermarkets.

Teff This tiny Ethiopian cereal grain (*Eragrostis tef*) is now being grown in the United States and has increasing availability in Ethiopian and natural food markets. Teff has a superior nutritional profile to other grass-family grains and takes only 15 minutes to cook. As a flour, it is excellent in pastries and quick breads.

Tempeh This fermented soy product, Indonesian in origin, is a versatile and nutritious food. When pan-fried, it substitutes nicely for fish, poultry or meat. Tempeh is available in Asian and natural food markets.

Triticale A high-protein cross of wheat and rye, triticale is available in natural food markets.

Udon A Japanese wheat pasta made from a soft wheat, udon is cut rather than extruded. It has a distinctive and pleasing flavor and texture.

Ume vinegar The rose-colored liquid that naturally occurs from a one-year plum pickling process has many culinary applications. Macrobiotic cooks value it for its medicinal properties. While ume vinegar is technically not a vinegar, for it contains salt, it nevertheless has a vinegar-like bite and may be substituted for vinegar and salt in recipes. Available in Oriental and natural food markets.

Unbleached white flour Refined flour which has not been treated with chlorine dioxide is called unbleached white flour. Bleaching removes the light yellow color and destroys the vitamin E content. Unbleached white flour, like white flour, is chemically enriched and aged.

Wasabi This Japanese "horseradish" has a similar bite and aroma to our horseradish. The root is rarely available fresh. Powdered wasabi is typically available in Oriental markets and some natural food stores. Authentic wasabi powder, when mixed with water, turns a dull green color. When adulterated wasabi is reconstituted it turns a bright green.

Wehani rice This long-grained, whole red rice is highly aromatic and flavorful. Wehani is available in some supermarkets and specialty food stores.

Zest The finely grated rind of citrus fruits enlivens many foods with a zesty, light flavor. Commercial citrus rinds contain toxic chemical colorants and pesticide residues. Organically grown fruits are therefore prefered for zest; they have seasonal availability in natural food stores. When organic citrus is available, make a zest supply. Remove only the colored portion of the peel, dry it until brittle, pulverize it in a blender, and store it in a jar with a tight-fitting lid. Then place it in a cool, dark place. Substitute one-half teaspoon of dried zest for one teaspoon of fresh zest.

Reference

1. Lumbreras, p. 39.
2. Heiser, p. 199.
3. Brody, p. 38.
4. Applegate, p. 68.
5. McNair, p. 16.
6. Applegate, p. 66.
7. McNair, p. 42.
8. Miller, p. 62.
9. Colbin, p. 169.
10. Miller, p. 71.
11. Harrison, p. 194.
12. Vietmeyer, *Science*, pp. 1379–1304.
13. Wilson, *The Herbalist*, pp. 115–120.
14. Vietmeyer, *International Wild Life*, p. 26.
15. Cusack, *The Ecologist*, p. 23.
16. White, p. 532.
17. Jones, p. 279.
18. Risi and Galwey, p. 164.
19. Cusack, op. cit., p. 27.
20. Juan, p. 304.
21. Browman, p. 116.
22. Ibid., p. 103.
23. McIntyre, p. 78.
24. Ibid., p. 84.
25. Ibid., p. 81.
26. Smith, *Southeastern Archaeology*, 4 (1), p. 51.
27. Underhill, p. 42.
28. Seeman and Wilson, p. 301.
29. Ibid., pp. 299–300.
30. Smith, *Southeastern Archaeology*, 4 (2), pp. 107–133.
31. Wilson and Heiser, p. 198.
32. Smith, *Emergent Horticultural Economies of the Eastern Woodlands*, pp. 26–38.
33. Valvilov, pp. 40–42.
34. Risi and Galwey, p. 155.
35. Browman, *Missouri Archaeologist*, in press.
36. Vietmeyer, *Underutilized Crops of the Andes*, in press.
37. Lumberas, p. 135.
38. Ibid.
39. McIntyre, p. 301.
40. Junge, p. 34.
41. Burland, p. 20.

42. Burland, pp. 115–116.
43. Tapia, p. 18.
44. Cusack, p. 29.
45. Paddleford, p. 32.
46. Vietmeyer, *Science*, p. 1379.
47. Johnson, p. 16.
48. Cusack, personal correspondence.

Bibliography

Adelson, Laurie and Takami, Bruce. *Weaving Traditions of Highland Bolivia.* Los Angeles: Craft and Folk Art Museum, 1979.

Applegate, Liz, Ph.D. "Winning Grains." *Runner's World,* October 1987, pp 66–71.

Appleton, Le Roy H. *American Indian Design and Decoration.* New York: Dover Publications, Inc. 1971.

Ballon, Emigdio. "Caracterizacion Fisico-Quimica de Diferentes Variedades de Quinus (*Chenopodium quinoa* willd.) Como Base Para la Seleccion de Genotipos." Universidad Nacional Instituto Colombiano Agropecuario ICA. Bogota, Colombia, 1981.

Banks, George. *Peru Before Pizarro.* New York: E. P. Dutton, 1977.

Bastien, Joseph W. and Donahue, John M., editors. *Health in the Andes.* St. Louis, MI: Washington University, 1981.

Bonner, Raymond. "Peru's War." *New Yorker Magazine,* (January 4) 1988.

Browman, David L. "Chenopodium Cultivation, Lacustrine Resources, and Fuel Usage at Chiripa, Bolivia." *Missouri Archaeologist,* Vol. 47, in press.

Browman, David L. "Historic Nutrition and Medicine in the Lake Titicaca Basin." Chapter 7, *Health in the Andes.* Edited by Joseph W. Bastien, Washington D.C.: American Anthropological Association, 1987.

Burland, C. A. *Peru under the Incas.* New York: G. P. Putnam's Sons, 1967.

Cusack, David F. Personal correspondence to Florence Magneron, June 3, 1984.

Cusack, David F. "Quinua: Grain of the Incas." *The Ecologist,* 14(1):21–31, 1984.

Duff, Gail. *The countryside Cookbook.* New York: Van Nostrand Reinhold Company, 1982.

Harrington, H. D. *Edible Native Plants of the Rocky Mountains.* Albuquerque, New Mexico: University of New Mexico Press, 1967.

Harrison, S. G., *et al. Oxford Book of Food Plants.* London: Oxford University Press, 1975.

Hazleton Laboratories America, Inc., Chemical and BioMedical Sciences Division. Analysis of Quinoa (*Chenopodium Quinoa* Willd). Sample number 71204859. Submitted December 17, 1987, Madison, Wisconsin.

Heiser, Charles B., Jr. *Of Plants and People.* Norman, OK: University of Oklahoma Press, 1985.

Hemming, John. *Machu Picchu.* New York: Newsweek Books, 1981.

Johnson, Richard. "The Legacy of David Cusack." *Denver Post Magazine*, May 4, 1986.

Jones, Tristan. *The Incredible Voyage.* New York: Avon Books, 1977.

Juan, Jorge and Ulloa, Antonia de. *A Voyage to South America.* Vol. 1. London: L. Davis and C. Dexiners, 1758. (Located in the Rare Books Room, Worlin Library, University of Colorado. Boulder, Colorado.)

Junge, Ingo. *Lupine and Quinoa Research and Development in Chile.* Concepcion, Chile: Escuela de Ingenieria, Universidad de Concepcion, July 1973.

Lanning, Edward P. *Peru Before the Incas.* Englewood Cliffs, NJ: Prentice-Hall, Inc., 1967.

Lappé, Frances Moore and Collins, Joseph. *World Hunger: 10 Myths.* San Francisco: Institute for Food and Development Policy, 1982.

Lumberas, Luis G., trans. Betty J. Eggers. *Peoples and Cultures of Ancient Peru.* Washington D.C.: Smithsonian Inst. Press, 1974.

Mahoney, Arthur W., Lopez, Javier G. and Hendricks, Deloy G. "An Evaluation of the Protein Quality of Quinoa." *Journal of Agricultural and Food Chemistry*, 23(2): 190–193, 1975.

McIntyre, Loren. *The Incredible Incas and Their Timeless Land.* Washington D.C.: National Geographic Society, 1975.

McNair, James. *Power Food.* San Francisco: Chronicle Books, 1986.

Paddleford, Clementine. "Kinoa, The Versatile Grain of Bolivia, Is Sampled Here." *New York Herald Tribune*, January, 6, 1945, p. 32.

Reichert, R. D., Tatarynovich, J. T. and Tyler, R. T. "Abrasive Dehulling of Quinoa (*Chenopodium quinoa*): Effect on Saponin Content as Determined by an Adapted Hemolytic Assay." *Cereal Chemistry* 63(6): 471–475, 1986.

Risi Carbone, J.J.M. *Adaptation of the Andean Grain Crop Quinoa for Cultivation in Britain.* Queens College, Cambridge, UK: 1986.

Risi C., J. and Galwey, N. W. "The *Chenopodium* Grains of the Andes: Inca Crops for Modern Agriculture." in *Advances in Applied Biology*, edited by T. H. Coaker, Vol. X. London: Academic Press, Inc. Ltd., 1984.

Seeman, Mark F. and Wilson, Hugh D. "The Food Potential of *Chenopodium* for the Prehistoric Midwest." Indiana Historical Society, *Prehistory Research Series*, VI, No. 2, 300–316, 1984.

Smith, Bruce D. *Chenopodium Berlandieri Ssp. Jonesianum:* Evidence for a Hopewellian Domesticate from Ash Cave, Ohio." *Southeastern Archaeology* 4(2):107–133, 1985.

Smith, Bruce D. "The Independent Domestication of Indigenous Seed-Bearing Plants in Eastern North America." in *Emergent Horticultural Economies of the Eastern Woodlands*, edited by William F. Keegan. Center for Archaeological Investigations, Occasional Paper No. 7. 1987. Southern Illinois University.

Smith, Bruce D. "The Role of *Chenopodium* as a Domesticate in Pre-Maize Garden Systems of the Eastern United States." *Southeastern Archaeology* 4(1): 51–72, 1985.

Takhtajan, Armen, trans. *Floristic Regions of the World*, Theodore J. Crovello. Berkley, CA: University of California Press, 1986.

Tapia, Salamon Chavez and Mateo, Nicholas. "The Andean Phytogenetic and Zoogenetic Resources." International Workshop on Mountain Agriculture and Crop Genetic Resources. Kathmandu, Nepal: Ministry of Agriculture, HMG, February 16–19, 1987.

Tapia, Salamon Chavez. *Prospectus for the Utilization and Processing of Andean Crops: Quinoa* (Chenopodium Quinoa *Willd*). Rutgers State University of New Jersey, New Brunswick, NJ: 1987.

Underhill, Ruth. *Autobiography of a Papago Woman.* New York: Holt, Rinehart, Winston, 1979.

Vavilov, N. I. Trans. K. Starr Chester. *Origin, Variation, Immunity and Breeding of Cultivated Plants.* Columbus, Ohio: Battelle Memorial Institute, 1951.

Vietmeyer, Noel D. "Lesser-Known Plants of Potential Use in Agriculture and Forestry." *Science* 232:1379–1384, 1986.

Vietmeyer, Noel D. "Gift of the Incas." *International Wild Life* 14(5): 25–28, 1984.

Vietmeyer, Noel D. *Underutilized Food Crops of the Andes*, in press.

Vilmorin-Andrieux, MM. *The Vegetable Garden*. Berkeley, California: Ten Speed Press, (Original edition, 1885.)

White, Philip L., *et al.* "Nutrient Content and Protein Quality of Quinua and Canihua, Edible Seed Products of the Andes Mountains." *Agricultural and Food Chemistry* 3(6): 531–534, 1955.

Wilson, Hugh D. "Domesticated *Chenopodium* of the Ozark Bluff Dwellers." *Economic Botany*, 35(2): 233–239, 1981.

Wilson, Hugh D. "*Chenopodium quinoa* Willd.: Variation and Relationships in Southern South America." *National Geographic Society Research Reports*. pp. 711–721, 1978.

Wilson, Hugh D. "Quinua Significant Past—Questionable Future." *The Herbalist*—A Publication of The Herb Society of America. 49: 115–120, 1983.

Wilson, Hugh D. and Heiser, Charles B., Jr. "The Origin and Evolutionary Relationships of 'Huauzontle' (*Chenopodium Nuttalliae* Safford), Domesticated Chenopod of Mexico." *American Journal of Botany*. 66(2): 198–206, 1979.

Zink, David D. *The Ancient Stones Speak*. New York: E. P. Dutton, 1979.

General Index

Recipe Index